INTERNET REVOLUTION: A GENERATIONAL STORY

INTERNET REVOLUTION:

A Generational Story

MARC JORGENSEN

ISBN: 978-1-7340548-0-4

Note on the Cover Art: The cover depicts a creative instrument (guitar) being superseded by digitally creative instruments (computers, laptops, smartphones, etc.) This represents the shift to digital instruments in the creative process. The cover was designed by Valeria Veléz Wolff, a graphic artist originally from Medellin, Colombia. Her art can be found here: https://valeriavelezwolff.myportfolio.com/

Interior page design and layout by Stephen Tiano, Book Designer (http://www.tianobookdesign.com/stiano@optonline.net)

"In the 1950s kids lost their innocence. They were liberated from their parents by well-paying jobs, cars, and lyrics in music that gave rise to a new term—the generation gap.

"In the 1960s, kids lost their authority. It was a decade of protest—church, state, and parents were all called into question and found wanting. Their authority was rejected, yet nothing ever replaced it.

"In the 1970s, kids lost their love. It was the decade of me-ism dominated by hyphenated words beginning with self. Self-image, Self-esteem, Self-assertion. ... It made for a lonely world.

"In the 1980s, kids lost their hope. Stripped of innocence, authority and love and plagued by the horror of a nuclear nightmare, large and growing numbers of this generation stopped believing in the future.

"In the 1990s kids lost their power to reason. Less and less were they taught the very basics of language, truth, and logic and they grew up with the irrationality of a postmodern world.

"In the new millennium, kids woke up and found out that somewhere in the midst of all this change, they had lost their imagination."

—Ravi Zacharias, in the 2000 book, RECAPTURE THE WONDER

CONTENTS

PREFACE

If you ask, "In your opinion, is the Internet making us smarter or dumber?" most people will hesitate to give you a straight answer.

One lawyer that I posed this question to reflected for a full 15 seconds before cautiously proceeding with saying "smarter." He then hedged his answer, describing how it is also making us dumber. An engineer at the World Bank, a development bank that lends money to countries all over the world, responded by observing that his parents' generation knew so much more detail about government policies compared with today's younger, information-saturated, generations.

Many people are quick to point out that the Internet has improved so many things, but struggle to confidently say that it is, in fact, making us smarter.

As an Internet immersed society, we do now appear ready for a more informed and nuanced understanding of the positive and negative impacts on our thinking, learning, social habits, attention spans, and politics brought on by the Internet.

People who were already adults when the Internet came about usually think harder about what the Internet has done because they know what it was like before. But younger people suspect things have changed and more often wonder how present conditions came to be. There are some people that grew up in the first wave of the Internet who may be uniquely qualified to see both sides because they experienced some of both worlds.

One objective of this book is to provide an insightful and objective account of what it was like for an average person to experience the Internet growing up. Another objective is attempting to answer the broader question of what the Internet did to this generation and how this will shape the future. Another objective of the book is to provide a practical record that could benefit some who did not live through these times. Another objective is to improve how people understand, think, and talk with each other about these changes.

KEY TECHNOLOGY DEVELOPMENTS OF THE INTERNET ERA

1. **1984: Apple Macintosh released**—popularized PC for an "average" person
2. **1986: Microsoft IPO**—created four billionaires and 10,000 millionaires.[1]
3. **1989: World Wide Web launches**—beginning of making the Internet accessible to an "average" person.
4. **1995: Netscape IPO**—stock moves from $14 to $75 in its first day of trading and modern Silicon Valley startup culture begins.
5. **1997: Google founded**
6. **2001: United States v. Microsoft; antitrust lawsuit leading to a decline in Microsoft's tech dominance.**
7. **2003: Facebook created**
8. **2007: iPhone released**
9. **2015: Cambridge Analytica data-breach**—triggered wave of backlash against social media and tech companies
10. **2019: Dept. of Justice initiates antitrust review of Amazon, Google, Facebook, and others**

---

[1] *New York Times,* May 29, 2005. https://www.nytimes.com/2005/05/29/business/yourmoney/the-microsoft-millionaires-come-of-age.html

KEY GEOPOLITICAL EVENTS SHAPING
THE POST-INTERNET WORLD

1. **1989–1991:** Collapse of Soviet Union
   Impact: Transformation of political and economic systems across the world. Embracing of free markets, liberal democracy, and globalization.
2. **Sep 11, 2001:** 9/11 Attacks
   Impact: Triggered global war on terror, including large-scale military operations and political reactions throughout the world
3. **2008–2010:** Global Financial Crisis
   Impact: Massive increase in publicly held debt and strengthening of the largest multinational corporations, altering politics.
4. **2016:** Populist/Anti-Elitist movements
   Impact: Brexit and rise of separatist movements and non-traditional candidates leveraging the Internet throughout the world (Duterte, Bolsonaro, etc.) changed relationship between the public, politicians, and media while also shifting sentiment away from globalization.

INTRODUCTION

THE LAST GENERATION WITHOUT A TELEVISION

Each generation discovers their own way to talk
Does each generation also discover how to listen?

In 2017, former President Bill Clinton tied his lifetime political success, and that of former President George W. Bush, to growing up without a TV. Clinton observed:

> "We were the last generation that was born without a television. I was 10 years old before we actually got a television. I grew up in a conversational culture, where people actually talked and listened to each other."[2]

There have now been three boomer US Presidents, born within weeks of each other other, at the very beginning of the Baby Boom.[3,4] Bill Clinton (1993–2001), George W. Bush (2001–2009), and Donald Trump (2016–) are each part of this last generation born in a home without a

---

[2] July 17, 2017. Spoken at an annual meeting at the Presidential Leadership Scholars. Quote between 30:00–31:30, https://www.youtube.com/watch?v=mhvw0Jrevqk

[3] The Baby Boomer generation is usually defined as 1946–1964, coinciding with the end of World War II (August 1945) and subsequent return to civilian life of large numbers of military personnel, leading to a sharp increase in the number of babies born.

[4] Bill Clinton, born August 19, 1946, George W. Bush, born July 6, 1946, Donald Trump, born June 6, 1946.

TV.[5] Since 1992, only Barack Obama, born in 1961, was able to win the presidency while coming from a different generation, Generation X. Since 1992, only Barack Obama (1961), from 2008, was able to win the presidency while coming from a different generation, Gen-X.

Once every few generations there's a technology that profoundly shapes the attitudes, behaviors, beliefs, and values of that generation and successive generations. The Baby Boomers grew up with television being the main technology that shaped their world during the crucial years of their youth and young adulthood. Television defined the prevailing economic, political, spiritual, and philosophical conditions for years to come. It helped define the perspectives during youth and young adulthood affecting both the actual and perceived reality of that generation, conditioning their generational character.

Today there is a new intergeneration; they are the last generation to remember living without the Internet. This book focuses on those born in the '80s through the early '90s, and specifically how the world altered (e.g., social, entertainment, business, personal, etc.) by our collective embrace of the Internet.

Contrary to most books on this topic that are written from th perspective of key leaders, this book is written from the perspective of an "average person."[6] Someone who used and experienced many of these changes first hand as a customer or user and what that looked and felt like.

There will be comparisons between the early Internet in its exciting immature forms and the current more mature format, which is referred to as "Internet Maturity."[7]

---

[5] Interestingly, three other recent presidential candidates were born within a year or two of Clinton, Bush, and Trump. Al Gore (1948), from 2000, Mitt Romney (1947), from 2012, and Hillary Clinton (1947) from 2016.

[6] The "average person" is defined here as someone who uses many of the popular internet websites, apps, and technology (e.g., Google, Facebook, podcasts, smartphones, etc.) but does not possess significant coding or advanced technical skills.

[7] "Internet Maturity" is defined in this book as the Internet reaching a point where the Internet is trusted and used nearly as much or more than real-life social or commercial interactions. Also, it involves merging real-world life with Internet life.

CHAPTER ONE

WHEN LETTERS MEANT SOMETHING

My High School sophomore English teacher, Mr. Kennedy, required our class to write and send out by mail a handwritten letter each week. It was the fall of 1997, but his classroom looked like it belonged in the '70s. The retro sci-fi posters on the wall and dated objects in the room were from a bygone era. It didn't have that imitation futuristic look of some public schools in the late '90s. Kennedy had been teaching for maybe 30 years and looked over 60 years old.

Every Monday we spent the first half of class handwriting our weekly letter. We wrote these at our desks, using a pen or pencil, manually erasing or using white-out for all our mistakes. If a student had bad penmanship or poor spelling, it showed.

Mr. Kennedy insisted that writing letters was a crucial skill that would pay dividends in our professional and personal future lives. He assured us that writing letters would give us a leg up in sending out future job applications and maintaining close correspondences.

After we turned in the letters, I remember seeing Mr. Kennedy staring bug-eyed as he held up each letter. Mr. Kennedy claimed that he only assessed the length of letters, not the content. He said this to alleviate student's worries that personal stuff they wrote to friends might be read by their teacher. His facial expressions belied a keen interest in what the coolest students and cutest girls were writing. It was hard to believe he didn't read some of the letters.

To my surprise, I enjoyed writing these letters. I enjoyed it because we could write to anyone. I mostly wrote to girls I had met or bands I was listening to. The previous summer I attended a youth camp and met some girls that I hoped to keep in contact with. These weekly letters were a great excuse.

Email had been around for a few years, but people still sent and responded to letters. At the time, it was only a small subset of people who used email and letters were still a primary means for long-distance communication. Mr. Kennedy made a serious effort to instill in us a belief that letters would remain essential.

Nearly everyone responded to the letters I sent, and this really surprised me. The girls I wrote sometimes responded with a letter and a picture. It should have been clear that the point of sending pictures to me was for me to send pictures back. But I was fairly oblivious and just responded with a letter. Not surprisingly, these correspondences tapered off after a few letters back and forth.

One of the bands that was part of the early '90s scene of Seattle music was a rock band called "The Posies." By 1997, I had started listening to their music. One Monday in class I was looking for someone to write to, and after seeing a fan mail address on the back of one of their CDs in my backpack, I decided to write to them. One of the singer-guitar players, Ken Stringfellow, responded with a short letter, which included a line saying: "This letter proves that The Posies actually do read and respond to their fan mail." As a teenager, getting any response from someone who seemed even a little famous was thrilling.

The most memorable response to those letters I sent out came from the CliffsNotes Company. CliffsNotes made those little black and yellow study books that were ubiquitous in high schools during the '90s. Students leaned heavily on these guidebooks for book reports and cramming before tests. Many students relied only on the Cliffs-Notes guide to understand or get the grade they needed for classics like *The Red Badge of Courage* or *The Scarlet Letter*.

One day, I urgently needed to find someone to send a letter and found a CliffsNotes guidebook in my backpack with a contact address. I wrote a letter, addressed it, and sent it off assuming they wouldn't respond. I was very surprised when, a week later, I received, not a letter, but a whole package from CliffsNotes in response. The package was loaded with pens, notepads, books, and, oddly enough, CliffsNotes-themed boxer shorts. The package also included a letter from the VP of Marketing at the company. In the letter, he said something that I never forgot: "Each week, we receive several letters from readers, but your letter certainly stood out."

Looking back, it may have been a modified letter template. But this response gave me some confidence in what letters could accomplish. It also seemed to affirm that a human touch mattered to people. When you received a letter it meant something and you felt it. Amidst all the junk mail piling up the personalized real letters stood out. Someone had taken the time to write down their thoughts on paper that they had touched, held, packaged and sent especially for you. You felt connected through letters in a way that digital communications still struggle to match. Communication through letters was a slower process, and consequently, you placed more value on what was said.

Sending letters was a slow process, so you had higher expectations. It was easier to focus on waiting for a response to a single letter because this was the only practical means to communicate long-distance. Long-distance calls were not an option since it cost too much. With our communications today, immediate text, video, and audio message options can sometimes make you feel impatient if you wait for more than a few minutes for a response.

Waiting for a letter was drawn out over days and unlike technology now, you were not sure if a delayed response was by choice or not. It was slow and focused anticipation. Waiting for email or text responses is usually hurried and fractures attention. A delayed response to a letter was socially acceptable, as it took much more time to write and send a letter. Ignoring or delaying a response to an email for more than a day may have social consequences depending on the circumstance.

Had I been in Mr. Kennedy's English class just a few years later, it's unlikely these positive letter exchanges would have occurred in the manner they did. Email quickly replaced letters and changed the nature of communication. Emails are faster, cheaper, and so much more convenient than letters.

Email gave us the first big behavioral change of the Internet age.

As with all major technology-driven change, the initial impact disorients our collective social fabric as all adjust to the new speeds made possible. This is often followed by waves of backlash, to get back to something more natural, during an adjustment period.

It can take generations for people to adapt to significant shifts in technology. As a technology becomes easier to use, more accessible to average people and more integrated with our daily lives, people use the technology in more natural and complementary ways. Then we can use the technology in more mature and effective ways. This is when we get the full range of benefits at the individual and societal levels.

CHAPTER TWO

THE '80s: LAST KIDS BORN WITHOUT COMPUTERS

"Children under the age of six, have a totally different relationship with technology than their older brothers and sisters ... I don't want to predict what that's going to do."[7]

    —Roger McNamee, Renowned Silicon Valley entrepreneur
    and investor

I was born in 1982 in Bellevue, Washington, a suburb of Seattle. Like most kids in my generation, my home had no computer when I was born. In 1984, my parents bought their first personal computer (PC). It was a Macintosh, Apple's first internationally successful PC.

The city of Bellevue is next door to Redmond, the location of Microsoft's global headquarters.[8] Inside Bellevue is an area called Medina, and this is where Microsoft co-founder Bill Gates lived.

In the late '70s and early '80s, Bellevue was mostly a quiet, middle-class residential area. Medina had summer homes for well off Seattle-ites and a small-town community atmosphere. During the mid-'80s, home prices began to increase significantly. High salaried tech workers with lucrative stock options at companies like Microsoft drove these

---

[7]Comment made by Roger McNamee during an interview with Emily Chang at the 5th Annual ITLG Innovation Summit in 2012. The entire interview was very instructive of the maturing of the Internet and Silicon Valley culture. https://www.youtube.com /watch?v=N2MPui3Y50A

[8]Microsoft's early headquarters was located in Bellevue and moved to Redmond in 1986, where it has remained since.

increases in home prices. Reactions to these changes were mixed. Some appreciated things like increased home values and others did not. Microsoft and other tech workers began to be both revered and resented.

In 1987 Bill Gates became a billionaire. A few years later in 1995 Gates would qualify as the world's wealthiest person. In the early '90s, construction cranes and large trucks at Gates' lakeside estate were visible from the 520 freeway and along Evergreen Point road, Medina's main street. Gates later hosted international celebrities, including Bono from the band U2 at this lakeside mansion.

Local news frequently mentioned Gates' estate, and both adults and kids talked about the cool things in the house they'd heard about, like remote activated heated flooring. As a kid, living about a 10-minute bike ride away from the construction site had special advantages. Whenever there were leftover building materials left out on the street, the construction workers would generously let us carry away small pieces of granite or plywood to build things, like a treehouse.

I remember people talking about Gates as if he were just another resident, albeit a very distinguished resident. People expressed a certain pride that one of the world's wealthiest individuals chose to live nearby.[10] But as I understand it, Gates had a limited presence in the community during the '80s and '90s, since he spent nearly all his waking hours at the office. Within the area, when people spoke of Gates they did so with a respect for his intellect, shrewd business sense, and wealth. Then followed this up with a joke about his nerdiness.

Microsoft collaborated with Apple in developing the Microsoft Word software for the original Macintosh. Working together early on paid off. Both companies were set on challenging the establishing order in the computer industry and succeeded. Despite this early success, it was followed by years of bitter rivalry.

---

[9] Gates, according to the Forbes list of the richest individuals maintained the richest man in the world status for most of the years in between 1995–2007.

[10] Interestingly, Jeff Bezos, who would, like Bill Gates, also take the title as the richest man in the world, also resides in Medina, Washington.

The Apple vs. Microsoft rivalry was an intense competition in the world of adults. But at the younger levels of society, on the playground and in public school classrooms, kids would argue about this as well. They disputed the advantages and disadvantages of Apple or Microsoft to the point that it was like an extension of your personal identity or like fighting over favorite sports teams, the Chicago Bulls or the Seattle Supersonics.

Steve Jobs co-founded Apple Computer in 1976, and by the early '80s the team at Apple had changed the trajectory of history by making the PC more accessible to the broader public. Apple products were attractive to large swaths of non-technical middle-class people whose first computer purchase was an Apple. With the popularization of the PC, it became normal for everyone to have a computer in their home.

Despite the breakthrough initial successes with Apple in the early '80s, significant market failures led to Jobs' removal from Apple in 1985. After mixed success with various projects away from Apple, Jobs would return years later in 1997.

Microsoft benefited tremendously through Gates' mother's pivotal connection with IBM executives,[11] which opened the door to Microsoft dominating software sales to large corporate clients. Once Microsoft became the industry standard, most large corporations followed suit. By the mid-'90s, Microsoft had a near-monopoly of the PC software market. And during the late '80s and the early '90s, Microsoft's success had eclipsed that of Apple.

In the late '90s, Microsoft had become the undisputed globally dominant tech company. During this period, few kids at school defended Apple. The argument usually went like this: "Apple products still look

---

[11] Bill Gate's mother, Mary Gates, was a board member at United Way America where John Opel, CEO of IBM, was also a board member. In 1980 Mary Gates discussed Microsoft with John Opel. At a later point when Microsoft was introduced to IBM executives, John Opel vouched for Mary Gates through his prior work at United Way. This connection led to a Microsoft-IBM partnership that was crucial early on: https://www.latimes.com/archives/la-xpm-1994-06-11-mn-2837-story.html

cooler" and the response: "Yeah, but you can't play any cool games on an Apple, so who cares?"

The success of Microsoft hinged on obtaining a near-monopoly of the enterprise (big company) software market. Microsoft also sold software packages that could be used on many different (lower-priced) computers.

However, since Apple designed its computers and software, the computers cost a lot more. Apple also did not have, at that time, the efficient supply chain it developed in the '00s, so its production was also limited. Apple computers were nicer looking but also much more expensive and fewer in selection than competitors. Computers were quite expensive back then. The competitive situation meant that buying an Apple was out of the price range of many potential buyers.

An estimated 10,000 millionaires were created after Microsoft made its Initial Public Offering (IPO) in 1986.[12] The company gave lucrative payouts in the form of stock options in lieu of higher salaries. The term "Microsoft Millionaire" came into common use, used in both admiration and derision. Many of them were in their 20s or 30s when they became millionaires. They often didn't dress, possess the typical social skills, or have the same sense of humor as most millionaires of the time.

The more Microsoft millionaires popped up, the image of what a millionaire looked and acted like changed. The image of a millionaire before this time was usually that of an older, well-dressed gentleman with superb social grace and elocution. Microsoft and Apple were the embodiment of this new wave of tech millionaires. They were younger, often unkempt, and although very bright, they talked in a way that most non-tech people struggled to understand. They came off more like the kind of guys you would see chatting away at a comic book store than schmoozing at a country club.

Nevertheless, because they had become millionaires at a young age, an aura of respect surrounded them. I would notice in later interactions with people, in places far away from Seattle, with people I met

---

[12] New York https://www.nytimes.com /2005/05/29/business/yourmoney/the-microsoft -millionaires-come-of-age.html

from China or Brazil, that people would associate anything related to Microsoft with being rich and smart.

For much of America, there was an idea that owning Microsoft stock was the best way to get rich. This idea of owning Microsoft stock making you rich became attractive to people who would otherwise never consider investing in stocks. My mom did not actively watch the stock market or business news. But she, like many others, bought Microsoft stock based on the attention and excitement surrounding the company.

In suburban Seattle during the '90s, Microsoft is where a lot of kids with nerdy proclivities aspired to work. Bill Gates was also the role model for aspiring millionaires and billionaires. Other billionaires, like Jeff Bezos, Steve Jobs, Mark Cuban, and Mark Zuckerberg would later surpass Gates in wealth and media attention. But throughout the '90s, it was Gates (not Steve Jobs) who embodied what people thought of as being smart, young, and amazingly wealthy.

Computers Everywhere

When I began elementary school in the late '80s, computers were beginning to be introduced into classrooms. Many school districts created computer focused initiatives and students had time set aside each week for computer instruction. Throughout the day, if a student did well or finished a task early, they got to use the computer to play a game. Students loved this game time. The game of choice was usually "Oregon Trail"[13] which was easily the most successful educational game that was actually fun.

Like most kids at the time, I thought computers were cool. But what I learned about computers came mostly from what my more tech-savvy friends showed me. This was because, at the time, most adults struggled with or had an outright aversion to computers, so they couldn't be much help.

In many classrooms, teachers who understood little about computers would assign that one kid in class who was always yakking away

[13]https://en.wikipedia.org/wiki/The_Oregon_Trail_(1985_video_game)

about some new computer game or a new fast processor to show the class how to do something new on a computer. Since these kids made teacher's lives much easier they were rewarded with extra free time and other freedoms to do whatever they wanted. It always seemed like each class had a couple of these kids.

For kids in the '80s, computers were exciting even though they didn't do much. Partly, it was because it was one topic where kids held the advantage over adults. In my friends' homes, I remember they always talked with their parents as equals when discussing computer problems or what computer to buy. It was all new information and kids could absorb and retain the information better. Consequently, it was the one topic where adults could not act authoritatively, regularly looking to kids for computer help.

At this same time that computers were introduced into class-rooms, they were being introduced into the workplace. In December 2017, at the Museum of Modern Art in New York, there was a display of photographs from the early '80s depicting the first experiences of office workers using computers full time. Aside from the distinctly '80s fashion sense, what stands out are the still, emotionless expressions on the young worker's faces. Seeing people with different hair-styles and clothing design, making the same mild face that we know well today, only made me see the similarity. Since then, screens have pervaded more and more of our lives and time spent staring at them with equally expressionless faces has only increased.

For most people, their first exposure to using computers began in academic or professional settings. As computers became more afford-able and offered more fun uses they began to be used more at home. Now, with smartphones, laptops, and broadband we are nearly always connected. But in the early years, when you used a computer it was in a fixed setting, usually at work or school. But as Microsoft and Apple computer products spread to homes and offices everywhere they were often unused or underused. Without the Internet, they were quite limited in what they offered.

In the '90s sitcom *Seinfeld*, you get a hint of what the computer experience was like for most people around this time. In most *Seinfeld* episodes you can clearly see a computer sitting on a desk in the corner of Jerry's apartment. The computer sits with the power off and is never mentioned. That's exactly how computers were for most people, much of the time, in much of the '90s. People had a computer, but they were like a piece of expensive furniture sitting on a table, powered off and lifeless, because it wasn't connected to other parts of your life.

To be sure, students used computers to type up papers and to play games like *Asteroids*, *Billiards*, *SimCity*, and other games I'll discuss in the Gaming section. Beyond these specific uses of work, school tasks, and gaming, computers were not a central part of most people's lives.

The Internet is really what brought computers to life because it allowed every computer, laptop, and smartphone to connect users with other people. So, instead of sitting unused most of the time in the corner, like in a *Seinfeld* episode, the Internet enabled computers to be integrated into our human social experience.

Between the early '80s and the early '00s computers went from being nonexistent to being present in every classroom and workplace. But it was the Internet that made us use these computers as they became essential to more aspects of our lives.

By 2007, when I formally entered the workforce, most jobs involved staring at a computer screen for much of the day. Screen staring was most common especially in entry-level jobs involving lots of data, communications, or repetitive administrative tasks. When you left work, you often returned home and began staring at a computer or TV. By 2010, once smartphones became popular, staring at screens was a near uninterrupted activity throughout your day.

The Internet Brings Life to Computers

Terms like "Cyberspace," "World Wide Web," and "The Information Superhighway" were thrown around interchangeably in the early years. People mixed up these terms all the time. It took years, but everyone gradually settled on "the Internet"[14] as a catchall term that was the best fit.

---

[14] The term "Internet" likely prevailed over alternatives like "Cyberspace" or "The Information Superhighway" because it was smoother to say.

The World Wide Web was created in 1989. This was a key development in making the Internet much easier to navigate for non-tech people. Before this the Internet was used by a small number of specialized academics, hackers, and computer hobbyists. Before the World Wide Web, very few people knew about or discussed the Internet.

In 1991 my Dad and older brother set up one of those infamously noisy dial-up modems. If you heard these old modems start, you never forgot the noise. Obnoxious static and beeping noise gave you a feeling of blasting off and venturing into an unknown cyber world the first time you heard it. But every time after that it just annoyed the crap out of you.[15]

The first service I remember was called "Prodigy," which was mostly setup for online shoppers. Prodigy was slow and the connection dropped all the time. It did have a few programs that were fun and oriented towards kids. Overall it just seemed like an online shopping mall built for middle-aged adults.

About a year later we started using America Online (AOL). It was a better platform with more fun options, like live chat rooms, games, news, entertainment, and sports. On AOL it was easier to find people with a unique set of interests. You could find people knowledgeable of hobbies like Japanese Manga comics, or learn about obscure things like developing bow staff skills.[16]

Early on, finding people or groups with less-common interests or knowledge was a critical distinguishing benefit of the Internet.[17] Mainstream TV, movies, books, and magazines were good for things with widespread appeal. However, if you had non-mainstream inter-

---

[15] Apparently, this old modem sound is a nostalgia kick for people. There's a 28 second YouTube video of the sound, and as of November 2019, it has over 10 million views! https://www.youtube.com/watch?v=gsNaR6FRuO0

[16] Shameless reference to the movie *Napoleon Dynamite* but this illustrates the point that the Internet eliminated barriers of time and space in finding/connecting all kinds of people.

[17] The concepts outlined here regarding the power of the Internet to bring together specialized interests and niche markets were influenced by ideas described in the 2006 book *The Long Tail* by Chris Anderson.

ests, or lived in a place where few people shared your interest in a band or activity, the Internet now opened up a world of people equally enthusiastic as you, and that was a big deal.

To be sure, most people were bored by about 95% of what they encountered online in their first times using it. But inevitably there would come a moment when you found that 5% of the content that genuinely mattered to you.

I saw moments when people first discovered how useful the Internet was to them, they would exclaim: "Wow! I found a bunch of information about an old TV show that I hadn't seen in years and couldn't find anywhere," or "I just talked with a few people on the Internet about a village my ancestors came from" or "I just found some really cheap flights to Europe!"

Steadily, more and more people realized that the Internet had information that was previously very hard to locate, and after the setup costs, it was essentially free to access. Slowly, respect for the Internet increased.

But remember, in these early days, to find all this stuff you had to go "online," and logon to AOL, Prodigy, or some poorly designed website with a bad layout. This meant sitting at a computer and watching the screen slowly downloading. When the modem would suddenly crash or someone accidentally picked up the phone, you would have to start all over again and hope you found where you were. The modem connection dropping from picking up a phone happened all the time, especially in a house with a lot of people.

It took a lot of patience and focus to get online and stay online. Slow modem speeds and frequent interruptions meant that people got bored and left to do something else. This was especially true when the weather was nice or the connection was particularly slow that day.

Today we don't think much about going "online" because we are frequently in a condition of constant uninterrupted connection to the Internet. But back in the day, you had to physically be sitting at a computer and plan your time to be online. Opening up multiple windows or quickly downloading items just wasn't an option. There was only so much you could do with the limited Internet and processor speed, so you had to be tactical with your time online.

In more recent years there has been some shift in how we view time spent online. In recent years we focus more on finding time to disconnect from the Internet as a form of digital detox. Because the Internet is constantly present, available, and a part of most people's day-to-day lives, people need to strategically plan out times to be "offline" for an extended period.

The Internet is now more interconnected with our lives and for many young people, they don't know life without the Internet. And for many of those that do remember life without the Internet, they seem to be losing the ability to remember or comprehend what it was like before the Internet.

For those born during and before the '70s, their social experience is a world of difference from those who grew up in and after the '90s. For the generation born in the '80s that remembers what it was like before and after the Internet, it may seem like they are caught between two worlds, the pre-Internet and the post-Internet.

Those born during the '80s I call the "In-Between" generation. Because they grew up "in between" the generations that grew up entirely without the Internet and the generations from the '90s and beyond that have and will grow up with the Internet.

Being "in-between" does have some benefits, like a unique ability to bridge the gap between living in the pre-Internet and post-Internet world. Because the Internet touches so many facets of our lives, this includes the altered ways in how we socialize, behave, learn, think, and act in the pre-Internet and post-Internet period.

CHAPTER THREE

Chatrooms: Where We Learned to Talk on the Internet

David Letterman: Would the Computer give me more than I'm getting?

Bill Gates: You could find other people who have the same unusual interests you do.

David Letterman: You mean the troubled loner chatroom on the Internet?

Bill Gates: Absolutely!

(Audience): [laughing]

—In 1995, Bill Gates explaining uses of the Internet
to David Letterman[18]

In the fall of 1994, due to a family move, I was in the 7th grade at West Middle School, located in Littleton, Colorado. West Middle School was in the Cherry Creek School District, a mostly suburban school district loaded with students from middle-class tract housing south of Denver. West Middle School was a large, sterile building that resembled the architecture of the high school in *Ferris Buehler's Day Off* or the schools in other John Hughes movies in the '80s.

I remember sitting in class watching a Channel One[19] news presentation about Internet chatrooms, something that was new to me. In the video, they interviewed teenagers around my age from all over the country. One kid was from Connecticut, another was in Florida,

---

[18] Interview on the *The Late Show with David Letterman* in 1995 https://www.youtube.com/watch?v=4Gx-o70q6s8

[19] Channel One news produced news broadcasts for K-12 public schools from 1989–2018. Some notable Channel One journalists during the '90s include Anderson Cooper and Lisa Ling. https://en.wikipedia.org/wiki/Channel_One_News

another from Texas, and they all spent hours typing away in chat rooms every day. The topics they chatted about were similar, regardless of where they lived. They talked about what teenagers like to talk about: music, movies, gossip, school, video games, family drama, and the anxieties of growing up.

Teenagers around my age were using these chat rooms almost every day to talk to other teenagers. As you heard them talk you could see there was some loneliness. Teenagers that were less connected socially were probably overrepresented in these early chatrooms. But the interactions seemed very positive. Also, the fact that people were all from different states indicated this wasn't just some short-term trend.

In late '94 it was only a thin slice of the teenage population using chatrooms. To go on a chatroom at the time, you had to: A) have a computer in your home that you could use mostly unsupervised, B) have enough tech-savvy to understand computers, or have friends or parents who did, and C) not have too many social distractions in real life.

In 1994 this was a small share of the teenage population. It was composed predominantly of teenagers living in middle-class suburban households who were not busy with sports or other social activities.

For those reading this that never used a chat room here is a brief description. Chatrooms worked similar to the group text chats people have on phones today. Except the people were mostly strangers. Everyone in the chatroom can simultaneously type in text that is then seen by everyone. Most people had a screen name or alias.[20] There was an ambiance of anonymity since you were mostly talking to strangers with fake names.

Chatrooms were very appealing to a small subset of people because they made it possible to find the kind of conversations that you wanted to have in real life. Chat platforms had lists of chat group names of sports teams, bands, video games, some news story, or whichever hot topic of the moment.

---

[20] Avatars and alias names were common on the early Internet before MySpace and Facebook made online personalities more transparent.

During the summer of 1994, just before I learned about cha-trooms, my family moved from Seattle to Denver. As is typical of mov-ing, I immediately lost my group of friends and social connections. After making this move to Denver, I was definitely a lot more inter-ested in chatrooms than if I had remained with my old group of friends back in Seattle.

Most adults and teachers at school didn't get chatrooms. Adults just gave puzzled looks as if the technology was from a different world. The confusion of older people was understandable since chatrooms were not geared towards them. The painfully slow dial-up modems (usually 24bit/per second, unimaginably slow by today's standards) and staring at weird avatar names, is not something most adults enjoyed.

Moreover, adults at that time had learned different patterns of socializing before the Internet. They had learned to socialize face-to-face or meeting people in the homes of friends. Teenagers had more free time and their minds could more easily learn and adapt to this new way of socializing with strangers.

A lot of chatroom talk was inane and repetitive. Early online trolls appeared, they would pop into a chatroom and say something ridiculous or promotional. In those early days, there was a Wild West feel in the chatrooms because there were few enforceable rules. You had only sparse, unreliable information on the people behind the avatar names. Knowing people's true identity was hard to pin down. I remember a friend at school at the time telling me about his cousin who was a woman in her twenties that according to him regularly pre-tended to be a teenage guy, and people in the chat rooms had no idea.

But the chats could often be exciting. Some of the coolest moments were when someone would share bits of news or insider tips.

On March 18, 1995, I was in a chatroom talking about something unrelated to sports when suddenly several chatters quickly posted multiple messages claiming, "Jordan is back!!!" and "Michael's com-ing back to basketball!" This was the moment when Michael Jordan announced his return to basketball a little over a year after retiring from basketball to play baseball.

In seconds, everyone in the chatroom understood what was happening; well before most news outlets had made the announcement. This was one of the moments where it seemed obvious that the Internet could quickly convey information people cared about. It became obvious to people in these chatrooms that this technology was going to be around for a long time.

This was long before Google, Facebook, Wikipedia, so chatrooms gave you a feeling of being part of a special well-informed community that had access to valuable information. Even though the information was often incomplete or untrue, you also got the best information, and before everyone else.

In hindsight, it makes perfect sense why chatrooms were one of the early popular uses of the Internet. What is something humans all over the world do all day, every day? Talk to other humans.

Chatroom Filtering

The process of actively filtering the people you interact with based on a shared interest seems normal now. This was actually a noteworthy change in the socialization patterns at the time. Instead of socializing through real-world groups like being in the same class at school, neighborhood, or being a part of the same club or sports team, people were electing for interactions based on shared interests.

Faced with so many chatroom themes (ex: Lakers Fans, Punk Rock Fans, Star Trek Fans, etc.) you had to filter through the chatroom options to find the best fit. This process of online filtering has, in turn, affected our real-life social behavior.

In the years since people began to mimic their online interactions in real-life. Specifically, people became more deliberate in choosing to interact with people based on mutual interests or beliefs. Social apps, job apps, dating apps, allow you to filter through hundreds of people based on the attributes you deem important. As people become more accustomed to having this ability to filter online our real-life interactions have come to reflect this online filtering.

Mutual interests have always been important to personal relationships. But chatrooms dramatically scaled up the number of social options you had and could filter. This allowed you to skip over real-life social barriers and steps to forming friendships of trust. In a way, it probably did contribute to people becoming shallow. Having shared interests became more essential than knowing more about the person behind those interests.

Chatrooms Before Pictures Voice

As a 13 or 14-year-old in 1995 and 1996, it was surprising just how quickly friendships formed in chatrooms. It became normal to regularly chat with someone after just a few days. You could even miss talking to someone if there was a day you didn't chat. At times, you could even expect to hear back from online chat friends more frequently than people in real life.

Since you never saw a picture or spoke verbally with people you chatted with, you had to imagine what the other person was like in real life. Digital photos, video phone calls, and long-distance phone calls were cost-prohibitive for most people.

Chatting with people you didn't see or hear favored those with strong imaginations and typing skills. Not surprisingly, the image that developed in your head of the other person exaggerated the positive. This was frequent in many Internet interactions. At the time, the Internet offered much less information than today. Your imagination played a bigger role in the early Internet.

Access to the Internet varied by geography, so your city, state, or country mattered a lot on whether you had the Internet and how socially acceptable it was to use the Internet. I remember seeing in the late 90s magazines publish lists of cities with the highest ratios of Internet users. San Francisco, Seattle, and cities on the west coast and east coast usually ranked the highest. Cities that had Universities with strong Engineering programs also did well. The cities that had high Internet adoption early on tended to also have economies that fared much better in the past 20 years.

Lucia, a friend from Cochabamba, Bolivia who came to study in the US in the early '00s, told me that she spent a lot of time in chat-

rooms in the late '90s. She told me that it was from watching old episodes of the *The Simpsons* that she learned English. With English, she
could chat with people from all over the world.

In those days there weren't many other people from Bolivia or
Latin America in the chatrooms. Consequently, most of the people she
interacted with were from other countries with higher Internet usage,
and they usually spoke English. It can be easy to forget how much
English dominated Internet content and discussion in the early years.
Since then, instant, and increasingly accurate, online language trans-
lation has made most languages very accessible.

She described those early years of chatroom friendships as being
very different from online friendships today. The number of people
online was much smaller at the time, so therefore people were less
replaceable. Once you found someone you connected with well you
continued chatting for much longer than is normal now. People who
connected well would type for hours, or days, even months. I heard
lots of stories of people chatting for years and becoming lifelong
friends. You shared life aspirations, frustrations, secrets, and ideas
with someone whose voice you had never heard and face you had
never seen.

The chat friendships in early online chatrooms more closely imitated how people were accustomed to treating people in friendships
at the time in real-life. In other words, people used the social skills
and behaviors that they learned from real-life experience and applied
them to the online social sphere. Now, much of people's social interactions are online so their social behavior in real-life mimics what they
learn online.

Internet culture now is arguably a greater influence on how people treat their real-life relationships than the reverse. Internet companies, and especially social media apps, have had exceptional influence
(both positive and negative) in shaping how people behave socially,
especially the younger generations.[21]

My friend Lucia told me that when she was in the early chatrooms
"it was strange not knowing what the person looked like after chatting

with them for a while." She went on "after getting to know the person better, you would ask to see a picture or arrange a time to talk with them on the phone. Sending a picture online took a lot of time. You had to go to a copy shop, pay to scan a picture and wait a long time as it slowly uploaded through a slow modem. And the pictures had a low pixel count and were very poor quality."

She continued, "to talk on the phone, you had to buy an international calling card, which for $5 would usually give you maybe 30 minutes of talking time." These phone calls could become awkward. The voice you started to hear on the phone was very different from the one you had heard in your head for months while in the chatroom.

International calling card prices came down a lot in the early '00s, perhaps because VoIP calling quality improved and people could use the Internet to make calls.

These early chatrooms created a small segment of people throughout the United States and the rest of the world who felt like the people they were most connected with didn't live in their own neighborhoods or even in their same city. The people with whom they felt most connected lived an 8-hour drive or $300 plane ticket away, or in a different country altogether.

In the early '00s, digital cameras became more affordable and standardized on laptops and phones. This made it so much easier to share pictures. Soon after it became more socially acceptable to share pictures. With a clear picture, people felt fewer barriers to interacting openly and transparently. Seeing pictures was more appealing for most people and this consequently broadened the range and immensely increased the number of people seeking online social interaction.

---

[21] Stanford's Persuasive Technology Lab (https://captology.stanford.edu/) has been influential in developing "captology" which, as it sounds, is the study of persuasive technology to capture and hold, people's attention. Lab alumni went on to influential roles at Facebook, Instagram, and other social media companies. Former Google ethicist, Tristan Harris, outlined some impacts of persuasive technologies at the Atlantic Council on Oct 8, 2018, https://www.youtube.com/watch?v=WGkmd7Tv6PU

Chatroom Summary

Looking back, it is clear that Chatrooms provided the social interaction that some people craved but it wasn't ideal for most. Fake names, avatars, and an environment of anonymity did not appeal to most people.[22] In a way chatrooms, conversations and friendships were a continuation of the kinds of interactions forged through letters for hundreds of years, just with a new technology medium. Pen pals had existed for many years.

However, online communications were very different from sending letters to pen pals since they were immediate while staring at glowing screens. Staring at screens probably has a more powerful effect of separating your mind from your body[23] and your immediate surroundings. In this state, your mind may be more easily seduced into thinking that all it needs is on the screen.

The Internet Starts Talking

One thing that is often overlooked in early Internet social interactions is the absence of voice. One reason for this may be that in the beginning, the Internet was very text and picture focused. Sound was nonexistent or poor quality so people didn't often use it.

In the early years of the Internet, people became more adept at typing rather than talking. Typing became a convenient way to respond to chats or emails quickly or at your leisure. Talking was also inconve-

---

[22] Anonymity on the Internet was a necessity for many early Internet pioneers. As the Internet became increasingly commercialized the early ethos of anonymity and anti-establishment fell out of fashion. Early Internet pioneers, such as Grateful Dead lyricist John Barlow, promoted an egalitarian vision of the Internet, seeking to protect the identity, rights, and access for each individual. The ultimate goal was to protect each person's thoughts, ideas, and rights to open access which could, in turn, open the door to allow any person anywhere to learn anything they want.

[23] This concept has received increased artistic attention in recent years. Passing through the Singapore International airport in 2018, I saw several art pieces depicting the ways the Internet and phones dominate our attention. The concept of separating your mind from your body is explored in-depth in the 2018 alternative rock album In The Future Your Body Will Be the Furthest Thing from Your Mind by Los Angeles-based band Failure.

nient because you were always typing at a computer, making the process less private and more complicated.

Beginning in the mid-'00s, Skype and other Voice over the Internet Protocol (VoIP) services made calls and video calls cheaper and easier. Despite the emergence of these new convenient methods, most people didn't use them often, except for talking to people outside the country.

People had become more comfortable with a digital layer between them and the person they were communicating. The generation born after the early 90s is much better at typing than talking, compared with those born in the 70s and 80s who are much more comfortable talking than typing.[24]

More Electronic-Mail

In the fall of 1996, I opened my first email account. It was a Hotmail account, the most popular email service at the time. Email had already been around for years, but it was mostly confined to professional settings. The mid-90s is when most high school, college students, and corporate workers got their first email accounts.

How frequently you checked your email depended on your social habits and comfort with technology. There was usually a group of students that used email all the time and they would respond to emails very fast. These were the students most attuned to technology and seemed like they preferred the Internet to real life. Friends I knew that were aspiring to be Microsoft millionaires would respond to emails quickly. At the time, Bill Gates was well known to respond to emails on the same day.

It was so exciting when you opened your first emails. But once the novelty of receiving an email wore off you stopped checking your email as regularly. And when people didn't check their email regularly it made the rhythm of communication awkward.

In those early years of email, there was no filter for SPAM emails. So your inbox would be regularly flooded with all kinds of spam, chain

---

[24] I expand on this idea in a later section titled **Textualized**.

emails, and other promotional junk that made you hate opening your inbox. Some email subject lines were strange:

"NEED A LIFE CHANGE? HERE'S THE SECRET NOBODY WILL TELL YOU!"

"STOP AGING NOW WITH SPECIAL ANTI-AGING MEDICATION NOW LEGALLY AVAILABLE IN THE UNITED STATES"

"SSSSSHHHHH ... Pass this along and something good will happen to you soon!!!"

Early email marketing illustrated the transition from traditional marketing to Internet marketing. Established mass mailing companies simply rolled over the same tactics used in traditional mass mailing to email marketing. So the SPAM and marketing emails that were written for someone 50+ would get sent to a 14-year old. You could tell by the movie references, expressions, and outdated vocabulary.

As a 14-year-old it was interesting to read these emails and figure out who the intended audience was because it was definitely not for someone young with no money. With the Internet today, tools have enabled much more efficient marketing segmentation. When you read some marketing email or social media ad, it's usually intended for someone roughly like you.

Over time, data and online marketing got much more precise. As the Internet matured data mining and extracting personal information became very important to Internet companies because it enabled targeted messaging and advertising. With loads of data, companies filter by interests and preferences in powerful ways to matchup potential customers with the right products.

The marketing of the '90s was developed during the era of mass media: radio, television, newspapers, and magazines. Alvin Toffler's book *The Third Wave* emphasizes how mass media put to great use with industrial era technologies like radio to capture the attention of the masses.

Big companies that could dominate newspapers, magazines, radio, and TV could convince the masses to buy certain products or hold an opinion if the message was catchy, direct, and repeated as long as the message was observed by the target audience. The main limitation was that there was no reliable way to ensure an intended potential consumer was listening or watching the advertisement. The solution was usually to spend a lot of money on bigger, louder, or more provocative advertising hoping it would get through.

The Internet era was such a break from the past because it broke this mass media advertising model as it solved the problem of filtering through and finding the right people for a message. Targeting and customizing messages to specific groups, subgroups, and individuals became cheaper and easier. You could also assess the effectiveness of a message much more easily.

One consequence of moving away from the era of mass media is that fewer products, TV shows, and ideas in the Internet era are intended to appeal to the masses. The Internet facilitates making money or finding relevance for an idea by targeting relatively small groups of people.

In recent years people more easily determine if an email ad, product, or even a TV show is intended for someone "like them". I have seen this especially true of those born after the early '90s. They look at an ad or TV show and then quickly judge its relevance for them. I remember one co-worker saying "I looked at the show description, and it didn't look like it was made for people like me, so I just ignored it."

By the year 2000 email was undisputed as the new official form of communication. Email marketing became more sophisticated and targeted. Many Universities and companies began making it the official form of communication by the early '00s. Since email, I don't think I ever sent more than a few personal letters.

Beyond Normal Intergenerational Differences in Social Habits
Generational differences in social habits, values, beliefs, attitudes are normal. There are expected differences due to growing up in a different time. But every so often the conditions are distinctly different

bringing about a more dramatic change or break with the past. The Internet is one such significant change bringing out more than the normal differences between generations.

In recent years many people have been trying to ascertain just how different the changes are between the generations that grew up with the Internet and those that grew up without. Some wonder if the differences are just normal. I have heard many people wrongly quote that even Socrates in Ancient Greece complained that "The children now love luxury, they have bad manners, contempt for authority ... " but this quote is wrongly attributed to Socrates and likely only made much more recently.[25]

Those of us growing up while the Internet was emerging were simultaneously developing real-world social habits and Internet social habits. One thing absent in online friendships and interactions was human expressions that couldn't be transferred through words on a screen. The tone of voice, the emphasis on words, accents, facial expressions, pauses in speech, looks of boredom, excitement for an idea, and so many other modes of body language.

Many of us in that first generation of Internet users, and more so in those born after the early '90s, never developed smooth in-person communication skills. Most born after the early '90s are more comfortable and expressive when communicating online than in person.

A large share of our social learning at a young age is occurring in part digital and part real life in a disjointed manner. This is more the case for those who grew up as the Internet matured (1990–2015). I argue that social learning is becoming more integrated and less disjointed.

There are always misunderstandings and tensions between generations. However, as the emergence of the Internet has caused a

---

[25]This quote was used by the Mayor of Amsterdam in 1966 following a street demonstration and reported in the New York Times on April 3, 1966. Although you still hear this quoted by journalists and politicians to support the claim that the older generation has always been worried about the younger generation, scholars have not traced this quote to Socrates. It has only been traced to sources within the past century. https://quoteinvestigator.com/2010/05/01/misbehave/

more significant break from the past in our social habits and values increased generational misunderstandings, tensions, blaming, and frustration should be expected.

Even for many born in the '80s and who used the Internet as teenagers, in our speech cadence, voice inflections, and facial expressions you can observe patterns of those who did most of their socializing online compared with those who socialized mostly in real life.

In 2017, Professor Camille Paglia commented that after teaching college students for decades she noticed recent years that student's "body language and facial expressions" were "becoming much more flat affect"[26] every year. Paglia attributed this to students, and people in general, becoming more accustomed to looking at screens than people.

Communicating online in the early years did feel a bit more detached from the real world. There was: A) fewer people online, B) most did not type well, and C) constantly staring at a screen up close was a new thing. Acronyms like "lol," "brb," and "ttyl" were being used for the first time. It takes some time for new words and expressions to be acquired into your vocabulary and be internalized for new Internet users.[27]

People in this first generation of the Internet never became as comfortable with the Internet as those born after the Internet. Those born in the '90s and '00s fully immersed in Internet culture can intuitively understand online communication methods like emojis, memes, abbreviations, and cadences of communication in ways that few in older generations will achieve.

For those born in the '80s, there was one clear advantage over those born in the '70s. Keyboard typing had been taught in schools for years. But, the difference is that when those born in the '80s reached

---

[26] "Modern Times: Camille Paglia & Jordan Peterson" Oct 2, 2017. Comment occurs at approximately 1:25:55–1:27:00, https://www.youtube.com/watch?v=v-hIVnmUdXM

[27] Subsequent generations would become much more effective in the use of emojis, GIFs and other online communications.

the age of 13 or 14, a key phase in the brain in social development,[28] many were using chat rooms or other online gaming that required typing skills learned in class. This was the first large cohort of kids who were using those typing skills for fun just as they learned them. For many kids born in the '70s, they learned to type but didn't have a social reason or necessity to use those typing skills until much later.

Typing skills of those born in the '80s were much better than those just a few years older. Many of us quickly became faster at typing than the adult teachers who taught us how to type. Our social skills probably suffered a bit, because it was disorientating going from the real-life, of seeing, reacting, and talking in person to one that just required reading and typing while staring at a screen.

For those born in the '70s, orthography was important and typing unnecessary until college. It wasn't until the late '90s when most High School teachers started requiring printed assignments. I remember some teachers emphasizing the importance of penmanship, and even sharing horror stories of the consequences of poor penmanship, like a patient dying because the nurses could not read the poor hand-writing of doctors prescription. But this effectively ended with my generation. Orthography, or penmanship, was an important professional and social skill to generations before me. But orthography hardly matters at all anymore.

In these early years, online socializing did feel like you were leaving the real world so it was normal to develop a new set of social skills. They were two different worlds, and there was a separation of how generations learned to socialize in each. Technology improvements have done a lot to diminish these differences between the generations and merge the online world and the real world.

Microsoft and Apple: Gifts to the Next Generation

In 1979, Microsoft moved from Albuquerque, New Mexico to Bellevue, Washington. This put the two most definitive tech companies of the

---

[28]Teenage years are a critical period for brain maturation. Research supporting this is in the book, *This Is Your Brain on Music*, Daniel J. Levitin, 2007.

modern era on the west coast. This was a big benefit to students in public schools at the time since both Apple and Microsoft understood the market for computers and computer products would grow significantly in the next generation.

Apple and Microsoft both put their products in front of as many kids in school as possible. Both created programs to gift or lease computers to public schools. It appeared to me that Microsoft was more strategic in targeting[29] future customers compared to Apple.

In the school year of 1991–1992, I was in 4th grade at Medina Elementary School. Our teacher, Jeanine Rogel, understood how technology was changing education and put in extra time obtaining grants to her classroom had the newest computers. Due to the dedicated efforts to go above and beyond our teacher we had several Apple IIes and a Macintosh LC in our classroom, not very common at the time.

Jeannine would later achieve national attention when her 4th grade class developed and marketed a software package that was presented at M.I.T.[30] Jeannine insisted on being called by her first name, to avoid conflicts from several years earlier when the parents of some students objected to Jeannine having her students call her "Ms." Rogel.

I spoke with Jeannine in the spring of 2019, and she made an interesting observation from her 47 years of teaching. She observed:

> "At the beginning of each school year, I made an effort to find out who these kids were and how to bring out their talents. During the 2004–2005 school year, I noticed there was something different about these kids. After some reflection, I figured it out, they had no attention spans."

---

[29] Perhaps Apple had more marketing and promotional money to throw around in those early years. Apple was wildly successful in the early 80s, before being later eclipsed by Microsoft. Additionally, Apple's strategy of selling to non-corporate clients may have compelled a more heavy investment in appealing to future customers outside the corporate sphere. In consequence, Microsoft may have been more careful with where and how they spent.

[30] An article on Jeannine's remarkable career in teaching: https://news.wsu.edu/2012/05/18/jeannine-rogel-retiring-after-47-years-of-teaching/

The timing of this observation is remarkable. These students she had in 4th grade, in 2004–05, would have been born in the mid-'90s. These were the same years as the Internet entered into popular use, especially in middle and upper-class households in strong tech cities. This was probably the first wave of kids who genuinely had no memories of life before the Internet.

As students in class, we did spend a lot of time learning on the computers gifted by Apple and Microsoft. Playing games like Oregon Trail was something we always got excited about. We did extra work in class to play Oregon Trail. We bragged about everything that went well on Oregon Trail. We watched each other play Oregon Trail and shared in the ups and downs of playing. Oregon Trail was one of those rare games that both boys and girls enjoyed equally.

Later on in high school, I again benefited directly from a gift from Microsoft. In the Bellevue School district there were several occupational education courses, and I chose Radio Broadcasting, since at 14 I had developed a keen interest in music and wanted to be on the radio.

In 1999, Microsoft made a generous gift to our radio and TV studio located on our High School campus. The gift made the studio appear more like a real TV studio, with better lighting, sound equipment, computers, and fancy chairs that made the studio look so cool.

During one week Microsoft actually sent in a professional film crew to our radio studio to record us doing our DJ work. They spent considerable time setting up video angles with fancy equipment. For the students, including myself, it was very cool having a camera crew who clearly knew what they were doing and having them record your every move in the studio.

There was a lighting guy, a camera guy, a director, and they all worked together saying things like "great, that was nice" or "alright we need a little more volume" and "can you face the light" as they stood in the side of the room. You could see their eyes light up and face widen in a professional manner as they calmly said "thank you" after filming a clip. Clearly, they were professionals. To a high school student, it felt like leaving school and entering the professional world.

After class, I would leave the radio studio and walk back into the regular High School environment. This was a letdown because the studio was a conduit to a bigger world. The high school world seemed more confined by administrators, teachers, and limited social structures. So Microsoft, with all its money, investments, and film crews represented a bigger and more interesting outside world.

CHAPTER FOUR

OUR EARLY INTERNET

Computer Labs Popping Up Everywhere

Bellevue High School was like many high schools around this time that converted old classrooms into computer labs. There were about 40 computers in the room, with groups of four computers placed on large tables joined together in what was called a "computer pod." Classes would occasionally come in throughout the day, usually to learn a new computer skill. During open periods and lunch, the lab was available to any student.

During lunch, the lab was about half full. About a third of the students who went there during lunch were those that always talked about computers, coding, gaming, or other geek-related topics. Another third of these students were those who were working frantically on a last-minute homework assignment. The rest were kids that didn't have any definite place to go during lunch.

On the days I did go to the computer lab I did sometimes use the time to get caught up on homework, but more often I just surfed the Internet. The coolest and most interesting information could be found online first, even if you had to sift through a lot of junk to find it. Finding the good stuff is what kept the Internet viable and interesting in those shaky and unpredictable early years.

Between 1997–1999 there were lots of websites for bands, artists, special interest sites, and random small businesses. These were almost all created by fans or individuals with a passion. The designs were often rudimentary but clearly made by someone who cared a lot about what they were doing and wanted the world to see it. A lack of UX design meant that most sites were not user-friendly.

46

These were fan pages, set up as a hobby and much of the Internet was like this early on. Most sites were not built for self-promotion or to quickly monetize visitors like most websites today.

Most of the content was heavy on text with some images and a little bit of low-quality sound or video content. By about 2000, you would see a lot more video and audio files popping up, but the quality was still poor, and very slow to download. Usually, you would just sit and read, because the images would take too long to download, and this couldn't keep most people engaged for very long.

Early Websites: More about Passion and Less about Professional Skill

In this period of the Internet going mainstream (roughly '97–'00), one could notice how websites went from being made by people who had little or no financial interest to those being built with ambitious aims and/or financial backing.

As a teenager, during this time it was clear that many of the websites were geared towards people around your age. Younger people had free time, interest, and patience for learning new technology. Since there was not as much money to be made on the Internet in the early years it was mostly teenagers and people in their early 20s that were creating and using most online content.

Before around 1998, most of the websites were side projects built by enthusiasts. Their passion was obvious, but you never knew what you were going to see. The website coloring schemes could be bright orange lettering with green background and red flashing notifications, basically awful to look at. And as for content, often after a few months of regularly posting new/interesting content, the creator lost enthusiasm for the website, got sidetracked, and the site became stagnant.

At this time corporations had a limited presence online. Their websites were so out of touch, it was laughable. You would see websites for reputable companies in the real world only to become the laughing stock of the Internet as they put up a website with ugly logos and weird color and layout. Many businesses learned an important lesson about the Internet in that sometimes it was better to have nothing online than to put up something horrible.

I am sure that behind the scenes during this time, there were thousands of awkward meetings between older and experienced executives and a young web designer questioning and arguing through what should be done about this "new Internet thing." Companies were always doing revamps and making updates to their websites. Some sites looked very elegant but were not at all efficient to use. It was obvious that many web designers got away with doing little despite getting paid a lot.

There was a shortage of trained talent. The number of qualified coders, web designers and graphic designers that had quality skills or experience was limited, and it showed. For months you would see "Website Under Construction" or "Website Coming Soon" on many websites, especially the home pages for businesses. A lot of websites were built that were unnecessary, perhaps due to the urgency companies felt to act fast.

The psychological and social effects were everywhere. As people used the Internet more, it also became more professional and a bigger source of revenue. It created lots of excitement for some people and at the same time anxiety in others. When a new technology grows as fast as the Internet did, it triggers a whole range of human emotions and responses.

The Internet had an unprecedented impact, so you saw the responses were in every facet of your life, personal, professional, academic. The prospects of unlimited access to information, gaming options, people to meet, places to see, and profits were absolutely thrilling! This inspired the nerds, gamers, socialites, and eager entrepreneurs[31] alike. It also attracted the curious and imaginative types hoping for greater global harmony and cooperation because of the perceived universality of the Internet.

---

[31] For most of the adults during the '90s, being free from the mental burden of the Cold War period drove a sense of global opportunity and optimism.

The excitement or anxiety you felt was roughly lined up with how much you believed the Internet would benefit you or people like you. Using the Internet required some technical skill, but not much, what's overlooked is that it also required human social adapting and curiosity. Having positive experience with many websites depended on your degree of personal enthusiasm since there could be great text and nice graphics but no new content or special reason for you to revisit the site. If you were a fan, you revisited a site if you remembered about it or maybe placed it in your bookmarks,[32] if you really liked it. But usually, you forgot about that website unless it was essential to your life.

Few websites, aside from community sites or shopping sites, sustained continual interest for most people. As the Internet developed, the companies that would end up dominating the Internet were those that could incentivize and drive repeat visits.

One thing from the late '90s that has all but disappeared is the website visitor counter at the bottom of every webpage. It was a cool feature, you could see the increase you made to this one website. But for websites that got little traffic, it's not exactly a good idea to remind everyone how few people actually visited.

In the cultural values of the early to mid-'90s, there was something cool and interesting about being 'alternative' or 'different' and finding something that few cared about. But this changed as the Internet became more popular and commercialized. Many of the first regular Internet users were the kinds of people that took some pride in being atypical from mainstream societal trends.

Counting and metrics are still a central feature of Internet success. YouTube views, the number of likes or reactions, comments, and

---

[32] It's hard to imagine now, but Bookmarks and recording specific website addresses used to heavily affect your Internet experience. Before Google text search was often unpredictable. Website algorithms changed frequently and it was hard to keep track where you found what and on which search engine. Beginning around 2003, most people felt confident that as long as they could remember just a couple words to capture the gist of a website, Google could find it.

shares on social media are important to us socially and important to the business operating them, they are influencing and amplifying certain aspects of how we behave socially.

The early metrics were limited in that they focused on visits and time spent on a site. But triggering emotions and causing interactions has rightly become the focus since these activities are more meaningful. Consequently, the website counter itself has disappeared or transitioned to measuring more meaningful activity.

From roughly 1998 onward, the Internet was rapidly commercialized. The websites popping up were less frequently created by fans and more often built by a startup company or professional web designer. Many of the Internet companies around this time were speculative ideas propped up by unrealistically optimistic or misled investors. This rapid proliferation of websites and the investment that followed is what became known as the .com bubble.[33]

With the .com boom of the late '90s investment in Internet-based business got far ahead of how people were using the Internet. Many .com businesses were aspirational in chasing after groups of customers that just didn't exist online yet. Some perhaps even figured that building a website alone meant that loads of loyal customers would just show up on their site. A sort of "if you build it, they will come"[34] attitude.

Most traditional brick and mortar businesses had built a core of loyal customers slowly over time. The Internet was more similar to real-life in this regard than many early on assumed.[35] In short many web businesses failed in the dot.com bubble burst simply because there were not, yet, enough customers online to sustain them. Many MBA graduates from top schools and Wall Street investors anticipated,

---

[33] Parts of this were informed by Robert Rubin's book, *In an Uncertain World*, 2003. For more insights on the .com bubble, ask a friend, relative, teacher, or co-worker who got caught up in the flurry of .com stock investment at the time.

[34] Reference to *Field of Dreams*, 1989 movie that appeals to the boomer generation.

[35] Amazon may be the best large Internet company example of this. Despite huge ambitions, the customer base grew only gradually over the years before achieving market dominance in many retail areas.

or hoped, a rapid societal shift would move transactions from retail stores to online websites. This shift did happen, but it was spread out over a couple of decades, not a couple of years.

Following notable flops such as Pets.com[36] investors were spooked by late 2000 and avoided anything Internet related. As investment dried up even more web startups found it harder to sustain their business models without investment or customers. This resulted in even more shutdowns and slower development of existing Internet companies.

A key observation of the .com boom and bubble bursting is that while there was a rapid growth of web business which dropped swiftly as investment dried up, Internet usage continued to grow steadily. In

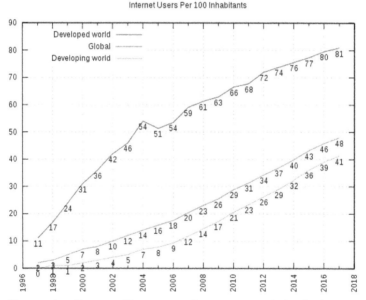

Internet Users Per 100 Inhabitants

Note continual increase of Internet users in 2000–2002, during the dotcom bubble burst. SOURCE: *Wikimedia Commons*, https://commons.wikimedia .org/wiki/File:Internet_users_per_100_inhabitants_ITU.svg

---

[36] You can read about this and other .com failures here: https://money.cnn.com/galleries /2010/technology/1003/gallery.dot_com_busts/2.html

other words, many startups and investors got ahead of where most people were at and their businesses failed, but people still continued to use the Internet almost as if nothing had happened.

That website visitor counter in the early years could earn you bragging rights. But in the climate following the .com bubble burst, a low visitor count became an embarrassing liability. Businesses wised up and began a steady course of less transparency and more control over metrics and data. Controlling data became essential to successful online businesses.[37]

The Internet Doubters

It's difficult to imagine now, but early on, it often appeared there were more Internet doubters than believers.[38] As mentioned previously, when most people started trying out the Internet there was a noticeable separation between those who soon saw its value for their life and those who saw little value. Enthusiasm roughly correlated with your level of tech-savvy and/or social needs. In other words, those who were more comfortable with technology saw a lot of fun to see, read, and learn about, and those who had busy social lives had little interest in talking to a bunch of strangers online.

Age was a big factor in how people viewed the Internet, but not always linear fashion or how you might assume. A key draw was social interaction, and younger people tended to be interested, initially at least, in broadening friendships and social connections. However, older people and those who were retired or otherwise had experienced a diminishment of social contact also had a keen interest in broadening their social connections. Hence, many of the early Internet enthusiasts were those most in need of social connection and these overrepresented people at both ends of the age spectrum.

---

[37] The most respected and valued tech companies succeeded in part with tight control and effective use information (Apple, Amazon, Microsoft, Google).

[38] Sun Microsystems co-founder and respected Venture Capitalist Vinod Khosla asserted that people often forget the early doubters of a certain technology after that technology achieves success. Comment made at Stanford Business School May 28, 2015, https://www.gsb.stanford.edu/insights/vinod-khosla-be-wary-stupid-advice

Throughout the '90s, you would encounter many adults who doubted the appeal of the Internet simply writing it off as another "fad." They would criticize it, saying: "people don't want to put any personal information online" or "it's too slow and boring" supported by their anecdotes of negative early experiences.

According to Kim Clark, Dean of Harvard Business School 1995–2005, Bill Gates was actually among those essentially writing off the Internet as something far less significant than it soon became.[39] According to Clark, during a speech in Boston in the '90s, Gates questioned the long-term viability and scalability of the Internet. Clark's also mentioned that Gate's underestimation of the Internet at the time likely contributed to positioning Microsoft at a competitive disadvantage in the late '90s. According to Clark, Microsoft "rallied" to improve their business and relevance in the age of the Internet, but "they almost missed it" Clark said.

In 2009, I recall hearing another person who spent his life in the '80s and '90s corporate world saying in effect "The tools the Internet provided in the '90s were useful, and an improvement on what I was using, but I am not sure it really could have benefitted most people in society."

Gates, an excellent coder who also possesses a deep knowledge of corporate business practices likely undervalued the benefits of making the Internet more accessible to broader swaths of society. Microsoft's monopolistic position in the marketplace during the '90s, Gates saw less opportunity in the unregulated environment of the early Internet. There was no easy answer to who owned or controlled the Internet. Web pages, chats, texts, and pictures were essentially unfiltered and without means to control. Gates likely saw limited opportunity for sustained profit in such an unregulated and immature environment.

As part of the boomer generation, Gates is an excellent example of many middle-aged, intelligent, and educated people during the '90s that just couldn't grasp what the online experience would unfold

---

[39] Kim Clark related this story about Gates during a student question and answer session in the Fall of 2006, when Clark was then President of BYU-Idaho in Rexburg, Idaho.

once large numbers of non-tech people began interacting online. Just as when telephones were first introduced, the more people you had using something the more valuable it became for everyone else.

Our Early Social Adaptations

The whole High School experience was changing quickly. Internet surfing, excessive gaming, talking with people at greater distances was mixing up the traditional High School social experience. People discussed this all the time. Teachers, parents, news reporters, people on the street, everyone was conscious of the change.

Whether driven by excitement or fear, expectations began to build up that things would change more rapidly than they actually did. Before the .com bubble burst, there was this pervasive, and unrealistic, impression that in just a few years the Internet would inevitably take over every aspect of our lives.

But if you were young around this time, you didn't really know anything different, so all you had to go off is what others who supposedly knew better said. There was plenty of fear-mongering from older generations and lots of horror stories about identity theft and other criminal activity online. Fellow High Schools could even be the ones talking down the Internet occasionally. Some avoided using the Internet for quite a while.

More Observing and Less Participating

The Internet increased exponentially the number of people to compare yourself, or to compare others, with. Comparing yourself with others leads to increased self-consciousness. Self-consciousness can lead to pressure to give off an allusion of perfection. A society with everyone feeling pressure to give off an allusion of perfection can be paralyzing. A paralyzing feeling can compel people to observe more and participate less. Not participating and only observing makes it easier to critique others. Criticizing others without the risk of participation is essentially empty because you have not morally earned the right to criticize if you have avoided the risk of being criticized by others. Therefore, the Internet facilitated less participation and more empty criticism.

This affected all people as they started spending more time online, but it was most acute among those who were younger. The generation born in the '80s that was coming of age during the '90s encountered a situation of being caught between the end of the pre-Internet era and the very beginning of the Internet era. The pre-Internet social skills that we learned growing up were phasing out. The early-Internet skills were not well established because the Internet tools were changing so frequently. This left us with one foot stepping into the Internet world and one foot stuck behind in the pre-Internet world.

One significant difference between then and now is the way going online separated you from the normal speeds of social communication. Self-taught coders and web designers built much of what you saw online in the '90s. It usually had the look, design, and feel of a place totally separate from real life. Some of those early designers probably had a more idealistic sense of building a little online world with their values and relishing having little oversight. As the Internet became more commercialized many of these early builders were forced to change to accommodate the more commercial or fade out of the scene.

The generation born in the '80s was taught to ignore boundaries. We were constantly told we could do whatever we want and that the main limitations were in our minds. "Follow your dreams," "Find your passion and pursue it" and similar phrases were repeated so often that for many of us it became the only socially acceptable thing to do.

International events also played a significant role. In 1991, The Soviet Union formally dissolved, ending nearly 50 years of a Cold War between Capitalist and Communist ideologies. The result was a momentous global victory for western-style capitalism, democracy, and open societies. In a few short years, political borders altered, market barriers dissolved, and numerous countries opened up to Western influence and business.

The Internet was timely because the thinking expressed in classrooms and conversations at the time was that since the Internet was a Western innovation it could be a powerful tool in extending this global unity, but with an obvious preference for western liberal free-market values.

The result of the zeitgeist of the times was that if you were to say that you had a dream to pursue one career but had opted for something more practical and 'realistic' you could be looked down on for not doing something more exciting, or with a meaningful societal impact. Between the end of the Cold War in 1991 and the 2008 global financial crisis and recession, there was a mood of limitless possibilities in the air. People gave less consideration to and talked less about the limitations on success, such as education and socio-economic background.[40]

Anyone can do anything is what everyone claimed at school, at sports practice, in movies, TV shows, all the time. The deluge of new information, provided by the Internet, fed into this notion that because anything was possible you were wrong to not try.

The economy grew in the '90s and so did the Internet. With youthful Internet millionaires on the covers of magazines the Internet became synonymous with endless possibilities, wealth, and the idea that if you could just imagine something, it could happen.

With the new access to all information, the expectations changed. The result of all this was that as the world was perceived to be more open in opportunities people became more critical in their judgments on those that were not pursuing their dream. These judgments were both outward and inward-focused.

Comparing, judging, gossiping is all very traditional human behavior. The fact that some young tech nerds had become rich then what was your excuse for not doing something like that?

Using the Internet had the effect of making the real-life you experienced every day seem inferior to an infinite number of alternatives

---

[40] According to the book *Freedom from Fear: The American People in Depression and War, 1929–1945* (Oxford History of the United States) the Great Depression brought about a heightened social awareness in recognizing the inequalities people faced in attaining well paid or meaningful employment. Following the 2008–2009 financial crisis, people may recall a similar increased economic awareness of social status and class. It changed how people talk about people's economic success. This increased awareness could also be associated with movements like "Occupy Wall Street" and post 2008 increased acceptance of socialism within the United States.

you could see online or imagine. In consequence, the effect was to make it easier for the activities of observing and judging since they became lower risk activities than participating.[41]

When Facebook emerged years later, it was significant because it actually put an accurate picture of yourself on the screen, and enhanced and reinforced your immediate social circle online. It made the Internet more personal and localized in significant ways. This was a vastly different Internet feel and experience from the "cyberspace"[42] realm of the early and mid-'90s. Facebook amplified the social experience online tremendously since it was fun and easy for regular people to use.

Bridging Reality

In 2017, while traveling in Sri Lanka, I met a girl from Japan named Yoko. We spent a day walking around an old Portuguese fort in Galle, located in the southwestern corner of the island nation. As we snapped photos, Yoko would take a look at the pictures and then process them through an app. When the app was done she examined it and exclaimed: "kawai!" which means "cute" in Japanese. I asked her "what does that app do?" She responded, "this app makes you beautiful."

I watched the photo in the app process and the eyes enlarged, the skin became shinier to the point of almost glowing, and while all the blemishes magically disappeared. Apps with these features have been in high demand.

Computer graphics during the '90s were heavily pixelated and poor quality. Consequently, you relied more on your imagination of what the Internet could do. The graphics and image processers have vastly improved since then.

---

[41] In the '80s and '90s you were barraged with constant advertising. Coca Cola vs. Pepsi, Reebok vs. Nike, AT&T vs. Sprint were constantly competing. Advertisers spent billions to convince people to feel good about their product choice and bad about competing products. Lingering effects of this were apparent in Microsoft vs. Apple animosity.

[42] "Cyberspace" denotes a separate world and was frequently used referring to the Internet early on. It declined in use in the 00s as the Internet became a more normal part of everyday life. https://trends.google.com/trends/explore?date=all&geo=US&q=%22Cyberspace%22

As the Internet and digital imaging have become more ingrained in our lives, especially for younger generations, we have a greater expectation to project an enhanced image of yourself. In consequence, there has been a backlash to people being compared to Internet enhanced images of others. More "authentic" and "real" portrayals of people are applauded.

CHAPTER FIVE

OUR COMMUNICATION CHANGED

The Death of Landlines

From January through April of 2004, I was on a semester break from college at BYU-Idaho. I decided to spend those four months with a company that recruited college students to sell home security systems door-to-door. San Diego was our territory for that winter. Going from the arctic-like air in January[43] of eastern Idaho, where BYU-Idaho is located, to the warm 70-degree days of San Diego was immediately rewarding.

During high school, I sold newspaper subscriptions door-to-door for *The Seattle Times*. Selling home security systems door-to-door seemed a bit harder but far more lucrative. Doing door-to-door sales involves these elements: walking to a house, knocking on the door, offering a polite greeting and then trying to hold the customers' attention long enough to make a sales pitch that they hopefully accept.

Since rejection is the norm, repeating this process for hours each day requires a strong effort in maintaining your mental and physical composure.

I left January 1st of 2004, making a 30-hour drive from Seattle to San Diego. The Oregon and California coastline are both amazing with spectacular breathtaking views that remind you how big the world is and how small you are.

While driving through California I called my sales manager from a gas station to get an update on arrival information. I remember him asking bluntly, "When are you getting a cell phone?"

---

[43] During winter months, Rexburg Idaho will not rise above freezing on most days.

A couple of days after arriving, I bought my first cell phone at a T-Mobile store in a strip mall in Vista California, not far from the Camp Pendleton Marine Base. The sales associate was very to the point. I took interest in a phone, she explained the monthly plans, and once I chose one, she just said, "Great, let's set it up right now" and rushed me over to sign the contract. She had probably sold quite a few phones to first-time buyers.

There were 10 guys on the sales team and all of us had to buy our first cell phone for this job. I had put off buying a cell phone mostly just to save money as a college student. But now the timing felt right, even overdue. It was 2004, I was 21 and it looked like most people my age already had cell phones. I also thought it would help me make some money with this sales job, or maybe would open business opportunities.[44] Above all, I thought having a cell phone would be fun.

The phone I chose was the Motorola V300, a cool phone in 2004. It had something that was not too common on phones at the time, a decent digital camera. It also had some very basic Internet functionality, which was called a WAP Browser. The WAP browser was awkward to use, but it did show short news and sports blurbs. The phone also had a few low-quality games and some cool sound effects.

After moving into our company provided apartments in Vista California, it became obvious to me, and the rest of the guys, that we would never again need a landline phone. The apartment had no landline unless you paid extra. Since the four of us had our own phone there was no reason to have a landline.

I moved out of that apartment four months later and never again saw a reason to have a landline phone in any place I lived. My physical address would keep changing, but getting a new phone number would be an extra cost and hassle with no real benefit.

For a lot of people around my age, we gave up on landline phones once we got cell phones. Of course, landlines do remain,[45] but they are

---

[44] I assumed that having a cell phone would enable some business idea that may have come my way. It seemed like the tool you were supposed to have.

[45] Unlike payphones, which are essentially gone and mostly just exist as an unsightly reminder to be removed from public areas.

much less personal and primarily used just in work or professional settings. Moreover, cell phones made payphones are almost completely extinct. The last mainstream movie to feature prominent use of payphones was *The Matrix* in 1999.

Disappearing Long Distance Fees

In 1972, before Apple was formed, Steve Jobs and Steve Wozniak sold "Blue Boxes." These were small devices that manipulated a payphone to call anywhere in the world for free. Using the Blue Box, Jobs and Wozniak made lots of prank calls, even on one occasion allegedly calling the Pope in Rome while pretending to be Henry Kissinger.[46] Early on hackers were focused on ways to make free phone calls. This may sound odd today since people don't talk about this now, but long-distance calling fees were an expensive barrier back in the day.

Today, the near absence of long-distance fees might not seem as significant. This might be because there have been so many improvements to communications since the time long distances fees disappeared (texting, video calls, etc.) that it just seems like one of many big changes. But at the time it was a big deal.

This widened the range of people you could talk to and, importantly, the length of time you could talk to them. For the '80s and much of the '90s the big phone companies, AT&T and Sprint, created a barrage of TV commercials convincing the public to use their service. They spent billions on expensive ad agencies and barraged the public with messages and endorsements from celebrity spokespeople.

Beginning in 1990, Candace Bergen, who starred in a popular '90s TV sitcom, *Murphy Brown*, was the spokesperson for the phone company Sprint. On every commercial, she looked you right in the eye while promising lower calling rates. AT&T responded with a campaign claiming Sprint did not live up to the low prices they claimed. The commercials featured a clever catchphrase: "Put it in writing."

---

[46]The Blue Box phone service was illegal and ultimately did not sell well. http://www.todayifoundout.com/index.php/2012/10/steve-jobs-first-business-was-selling-blue-boxes-that-allowed-users-to-get-free-phone-service-illegally/

The Sprint vs AT&T rivalry echoed another '80s ad war between Coca Cola and Pepsi. Kids would take sides arguing over which soda was better or cooler to drink. Your cola choice mattered to people since it said something about your identity.

But when it came to phone services, nobody really cared enough to defend their phone company. So, when phone fees did disappear, nobody had any attachment that bound them to any phone company. Or if they did, people forgot about it quickly.

In the late '90s, cell phone plans, perhaps to entice customers, offered cheaper long-distance rates. And by the time I bought my first cell phone in 2004, I remember asking, "And how much do long distance phone calls cost?" The girl doing the sale just gave me a strange look, shook her head and replied curtly, "Oh, you can call anywhere, there's no long distance." I thought, "No long distance, seriously?"

Area codes became a standard part of your phone number and it was now perfectly normal for most people in your phone to have different area codes. During my college years, most people were from somewhere else. You entered everyone's phone number into your phone by name and dialing got quicker. It also got more personal, since you called a name, not just a number.

With free long distance, people talked more frequently and for a longer length of time. Keeping in touch with family and friends in your city or at a distance became so much easier. It seemed like most girls I knew in college talked with their mom almost every day. Consequently, the mental distance between places shrank.

Interestingly, the ease of calling also made it easier to decide who you really wanted to talk to. I remember talking to a former roommate after a few months of going our separate ways and thinking how hard it was to talk to each other without the shared day-to-day experiences to discuss. In other words, you quickly realized after a phone call, which relationships could be and should be maintained.

Cell Phones Made It Easier to Avoid Talking

Screening calls wasn't new, by the late '90s many phones had a caller I.D system and people ignored calls from suspicious numbers. But when everyone began to automatically see the name or number of each caller it became much easier to avoid answering calls from people.

Part of what made it so easy to ignore people was the binary choice that cell phones displayed when you received a call. Your phone showed two seemingly equal options, one button to accept and one button to reject. It was like accepting or rejecting were now both equally socially acceptable options.

One of the sales guys I worked with in San Diego, David Kwan, reused over and over the same joke about choosing to accept or reject calls. He would answer the call with the same low-toned mock philosophical voice and say, "The name Marc Jorgensen, flashes on my phone, I have a choice to accept or reject it, I choose to accept it." It was funny, at least for the first few times, but he reused the joke so many times it lost meaning. New technology stretched the limits of what we would say to people when the cost of communications was lowered and the person was not right in front of you.

It was not just the cool kids who rejected calls, but everyone. People had a new feeling of empowerment by not needing to accept calls. Rejecting was a valid response and it became more common. You were not automatically expected to answer your phone, and this quickly changed how we spoke and interacted. Psychologically, it hurt when people didn't accept your call since you basically knew you were being ignored.

Over time, screening calls reduced the value of phone calls as people wouldn't bother making a call they knew was likely to be ignored. The quality of talking on the phone also reduced as people felt less need to be engaged with the call. People now understood that accepting a call was a choice, not an obligation, and they also had the option to actively engage in the call. Getting someone to speak on the phone required conscious effort.

Textualized

It was during the late '90s and early '00s when most people acquired their first cell phones (pre-smartphones). Initially, we were excited to just call up friends and talk. At the time, talking with someone on the phone was natural, because everyone grew up talking to each other. Phone conversations went much more smoothly than they do now.

Texting, in my view, was a big part of what made talking less smooth. Beginning slowly in the late '90s and early '00s,[47] people started using the short message service (SMS—texting) on their phones. Texting began replacing calling, and soon fundamentally changed the rhythm and pattern of our communication.

At first, typing on those pre-smartphone keypads was awkward. You had to press a number that was tied to three of four letters on the keypad. You did this manually for each letter. It was slow and there were lots of typos.

During the winter of 2004, the sales team that I worked for would talk to each other to pump each other up throughout the day and to cope with rejection. We shared success stories, jokes, and trash talk with each other every day through text.

Typing out these messages on the old numeric keypads, which had three to four letters mapped to each number, was a painstaking process since the predictive software would usually auto fill in the wrong word. To help with this, the predictive text software could also learn new words. Our sales manager, Ken, was thrilled to tell us, "I taught my phone to use the word 'Kwan!" the sales team guy notorious for making the sales team get home late.

Texts were excellent for group updates. So much easier than calling each person, getting them on the phone, interrupting whatever they were doing for a quick phone call. But, it could be slow if you needed an immediate response or an answer to a more complex question.

Between 2004–2006, I noticed that girls were responding more often through text than phone calls. In early 2006, one girl who I was

---

[47]Nokia made text messaging available on cell phones in 1993, but as few phones had adaptable keypads with corresponding letters, people were slow to adopt the service, making "initial SMS growth was slow." In 1999, texts began to be exchanged between networks, and this made SMS began to come into much wider usage. "A Brief History of Text Messaging," Mashable Sep 21, 2012. https://mashable.com/2012/09/21/text-messaging-history /#QH90tyiOnZq3

trying to set up a date with finally responded via text after I had called her a few times throughout the day (something not as uncommon back then). Her text read, "Marc, sorry I have been unable to answer your calls, I have two jobs to work today, and I have been constantly busy. I can't talk on the phone but I can text." Texting was overtaking calling as the preferred method of communication.

Around this same time, I remember when my younger brother Dane, who was born in 1986, going off on a rant against texting. He said essentially, "It's a waste of time. It's inconvenient and takes longer to send a message and a lot less effective than just making a phone call." I had been using texting for a couple years and defended texting, saying, "It is actually very convenient when you're in a meeting or place that you can't talk or if you need to text the same message to a bunch of people." My brother shot back, "If they don't answer you, then they obviously don't think your call is important enough, and won't listen to you anyway, a call is always better."

But the tide was turning in favor of texting and surviving socially without texting was becoming impossible.

A few years later in 2009, I lived in Tempe, Arizona, right next to Arizona State University. My roommate Dave was 24 and his girlfriend Vanessa was 21. After they dated for a few months, Vanessa left Arizona to go to school at Brigham Young University, in Provo, Utah. Provo, Utah is about 12 hours by car from Tempe, so, not surprisingly, the distance put a major strain on her relationship with Dave.

I remember Dave would say things like, "Man, it's hard to keep talking when Vanessa is so far away." I then asked him, "So, how much do you guys usually talk on the phone?" He responded, "We really don't talk that much on the phone; we usually just text. Even when she was here, we normally just sent text messages to each other."

That was when it became obvious to me the extent to which texting had substituted phone calls. It also seemed apparent that in dating relationships texting was preferred to calling because there was a decreasing level of intimacy in relationships and society generally. Texting provided a cushy layer of protection where true intentions could more easily be obscured, avoided, and managed. This was often under the pretense of protecting feelings and usually resulted in greatly limiting intimacy.

Getting back to my brother, that strong opinion he had back in 2006 changed completely within several years. By 2015 he was communicating mostly via text message. What caused the change? Between 2006 and 2015 he spent a lot more time hanging out, talking with, and dating girls. It had become an absolute social necessity for guys to text during this period, it was a sink or swim situation.

In general, girls texted more frequently and sent higher quality messages than guys. They created more entertaining and funny responses. Guys could learn and some became quite adept at sending texts, but for many, it was like learning a foreign language and they learned just enough to get by.

Replacing Note Passing

Sending text messages (and instant messaging) is a bit like what passing notes at school were to my generation. In the mid-'90s, when I was in middle school, girls would secretly pass notes to each other in class all day, every day. I remember one girl in a 7th-grade class named Alicia, who would whisper to me, "Write me a note," every day as she walked in and sat down at her desk. Every class turned into this fun game of passing notes back and forth across the room, all while making sure the teacher was unaware of the little folded up papers with short messages being passed back and forth across the room.

Just like texting, passing notes broke up the tedium of classwork. The notes were usually about what you did the day before, who did you have a crush on, something stupid a kid in class had said or done, and random gossip. It was largely the same things people talk about, text about, and instant message about. Technology may change swiftly but people, and what they want to talk about, don't change nearly as fast.

A big difference between passing notes and sending texting or instant messaging is the speed and viral potential of texting vs manual communications. By around 2010, sharing stupid text responses or funny texts became very common. We have all seen embarrassing and hilarious texts sent to us by friends or posted on social media. This is great for getting more laughs but also a much higher potential for damage as if an embarrassing message gets spread.

Uncomfortable with Calling

By 2017, voice calls were far less common than texts. There is a definite difference between those who grew up from the early '90s and after. I had a roommate named Mark, who was born in 1990 explain it like this:

> "Texting is so much easier than calling. With texts, I can take time to understand the message and then control my response. I can show my draft response to friends and make sure the response is appropriate. On the phone, it is a lot harder to come up with the right response in the moment."

Mark continued, "If I'm not ready to talk on the phone and I get a call, I just ignore the call, and then call back five minutes later when I'm mentally ready to talk." It did seem that the more popular texting became the less comfortable people became with phone calls and other verbal communications.

There is a mental barrier with people that didn't exist before texting, for younger people especially, to work up some focus to talk. Maybe people just got out of habit with verbal communications when most communications shifted to typed words.

Speaking appears to be less of a natural of a process for those born after the '90s than those born before the early '90s. Perhaps the reason is simple; people who grew up communicating through the Internet just had less practice speaking on the phone or in person. And those born before the early '90s had a chance to develop language and communications patterns while their brains were developing those areas involved with language.

It does appear, worldwide, to exist a defined separation between those born after the early '90s (later or earlier depending on when the

Internet became influential in their country) are far less comfortable with verbal than with text communications. But if you switch the perspective, most of those born before the early '90s are not quite as adept at communicating with text messaging (and other typed Internet-enabled communications) as those born after the early '90s.

It is responding in the moment that makes real-time verbal conversation hard. Since communication in person is two-directional, coming up with the appropriate responses with the right timing is difficult without extensive practice and natural experience.

Declining verbal communications are probably due to a diminished ability to listen, process the information, and knowing how to appropriately respond.

The generation born after the '90s became accustomed to huge amounts of information coming at them. Most of the time this information was observed while alone and staring at a screen. Staring at a computer screen requires no verbal response or any other immediate response for that matter.

The shift towards texting made it easier to replace spontaneous responses in conversation with responses that were controlled and carefully vetted. But in real-time conversations, you just don't have the time to control and vet responses as you do with texting.

Perhaps as a response to this people began to use phrases like, "I need to be more present" or "It's all about living in the moment" to show they could train themselves to ignore technological distractions and actually pay full attention to someone or something.

I was a radio DJ in high shool and I learned that rule #1 in radio and TV broadcasting is "no dead air," which basically means that anything is better than silence when you're on the air. This trained me to always have something to say. I also developed a decent radio voice. For years I kept that radio voice. People tended to listen when I talked. I knew when to change up the tone or pace when people appeared a little bored. This experience made me pay more attention to voice. And this also helped me observe how voice compared with became less emphasized in communications over the years.

New Phone Etiquette

By 2011, people were becoming so accustomed to typing and looking at words, pictures, and videos on their phones that it became harder to get people to use the phone to talk. By this time actually calling someone on the phone was, in fact, asking a lot, because you were asking them to actually focus their attention for a potentially open-ended time. There was a whole new set of social etiquette for phone calls. This was a struggle for a lot of young people that were becoming more attached to all the fun apps on their phones. You expected the first call you made to go to voicemail. If they didn't call back in about five minutes you called again.

I remember sitting in a group of about 200 single people in their 20s during a hot afternoon in Scottsdale, Arizona. A guy who was a manager of car sales and had put a lot of thought into modern communication behavior explained the state of phone etiquette at the time:

> "So, a few days ago, I called someone and after it went to voicemail I didn't leave a message. Now, we all know that when someone calls you and they don't leave a message, it simply means, 'Call me back.' I then waited for about 20 minutes and got no response. So I called again and left a voicemail, which as we all know means, 'Call me back now! This is urgent.' About ten minutes later I finally got a callback and I asked if they had checked the voicemail, and, as has become normal now, they said no, they just knew to call me back because a voicemail meant that I needed to respond as soon as possible."

This is how a lot of communications went at this time. People usually ignored the first phone call, and unless there was a voicemail, we treated the call as less important. If there was a voicemail, we usually called back, often not even checking the voicemail.

This is another good example of how people were shifting away from listening. It also shows that real-time talking over the phone decreased as all other forms of real-time digital communication increased.

Texting Across the World

In 2013 I lived in Washington DC and I made friends with a Chinese graduate student named Sophie. I met her at a Chinese New Year celebration at a friend's house. A few days later I messaged her on Facebook. Soon after Sophie introduced me to a messaging app called "WeChat," which Chinese graduate students were using a lot more than Facebook.

WeChat is similar to WhatsApp, in that it allows you to send unlimited text, audio, and video messages. The main value of these messaging apps compared with regular texting is that you can send unlimited messages to people anywhere in the world, regardless of their phone plan.

By 2012 everyone was texting all the time, so the timing of these messaging apps was perfect. Younger people and students sent and received dozens of text messages every day. Most cell phone plans didn't offer enough data for the daily deluge of words, pictures, funny memes, gifs, shared videos, and nonstop links to articles with eye-catching headlines.

Sophie was born in 1990 and part of a generational cohort of Chinese that took advantage of dramatic economic growth in China. China's rapid economic advancement began in the early '80s but kicked into high gear in the '90s after the fall of the Soviet Union.

The collapse of the Soviet Union in 1991 was a major global catalyst for socialist governments around the world to change and adopt new policies. In the case of China, it compelled leadership in Beijing to reevaluate and restructure. A key driving interest at play was self-preservation, as party leadership studied the history of many regimes and determined that to remain viable adaptation to new realities was inevitable for long-term survival.

This cohort that was born after 1990 spoke English far better[48] than those born just a few years earlier.[49] This cohort also brought a

---

[48]Technology and an influx of native English teachers from the US, UK, and Australia to China facilitated improvements in English language instruction in China in the '90s.

[49]I speculate that a big factor was also greater access to native English entertainment and media in the '90s and '00s than in the '80s.

huge wave of Chinese students who went to study in the US and Europe, mostly quantitative disciplines and mostly in graduate schools. Just like most people born in 1990 and after, Sophie was far more comfortable texting than talking.

I remember walking around the Washington, DC neighborhood of Georgetown on a characteristically hot and humid summer evening. Sophie kept speaking into her phone and then listening to recorded messages. The messages made her smile and laugh about something. I found out later that she was sending and receiving audio messages on a new voice messaging service through WeChat.

Audio messaging was slowly rolled out for WhatsApp, Facebook, and through regular text messaging during the next couple of years. Audio messages were especially useful for sending longer or more nuanced messages. They were also much better when talking with someone with whom you shared greater closeness or intima

Similar to texting, voice messages still allowed the advantage of better controlling and delaying response. For voice recordings, you could think up a response, record it, and delete and try again if you didn't like it.

One reason that voice messages caught on quickly with Chinese and other non-English speaking people is that it was easier to speak than type out Chinese characters on a keyboard that was designed for a Latinized alphabet. Moreover, was also easier to tones of expression, which is important in Mandarin and other non-English languages.

Chat Groups

Around this time group chats popped up everywhere. WeChat, WhatsApp, and later Facebook all had features that made it easy to create group chats. Friends organizing a trip, or a game night, or a work lunch group all became easier to accomplish. Chat groups were fun and easier than multiple texts and phone calls.

When using a social app like WeChat or Facebook, the group chats were more fun. Maybe it was because the apps were the first to put out the newest funny gifs and emojis or people also felt safe saying whatever since the apps were built to encourage person-to-person connection. They could also be more secretive, lots of people complain about secret chat groups set up to talk trash about co-workers and share other insider information.

By 2014, I noticed people were using group chats for regular long-term talking. My girlfriend at the time was from Changsha, China. She was born in 1990 and came to the US for graduate school. After she graduated in May of 2014, she remained in Washington, DC for work.

While she was in Washington, DC, her brother was studying in Seattle while her parents were in Changsha, China. They had a family chat group where they would post updates to each other, usually sending texts, sometimes sending voice messages or pictures. It replaced phone communication almost completely. They rarely spoke on the phone.

One thing that surprised me was the degree of private information being shared in the chat group. When her dad received a diagnosis of throat cancer he even sent a copy of his legal will to the WeChat group chat. The same group chat that was used to send regular updates or coordinate travel plans was also used for communications about serious life and death matters.

For families and friendships that were stretched out across the world, the chat groups became a vital means to cheaply and easily stay in touch. Naturally, families and friends separated by long distances were some of the first to take full advantage of group chats. But soon everyone was using them.

CHAPTER SIX

OUR IPHONES

"Living inside a screen seems like absolute freedom sometimes, but it's more like a kind of psychic decapitation... We exist in an era where the most primitive structures in our brains are being rewarded and controlled, almost constantly, by extremely sophisticated, interconnected, and self-perpetuating technologies. Everything is talking to everything else but there's no communication anymore ... "
—Greg Edwards, of the Los Angeles-based alternative rock band Failure, commenting on the impact of the Internet

Following the popularization of the iPhone in 2007, the changes to social habits were noticeable and fast. Initially, it did not receive as much attention.[50] It's now become quite common to discuss with friends how things changed since the iPhone since it has become such an obvious influence in the world we live.[51]

Text messages, recorded voice, and video messages became so much easier, and fun, to send with the iPhone. This altered how we perceived time. It also made everything and everyone feel more immediately accessible but at the same time more distant from the people with whom you shared a crowded room.

---

[50]The social changes caused by the iPhone likely received less attention in the first several years of usage 2007–2010 in part because the US, and much of the world, was experiencing the worst recession in generations. During these years economic conditions and employment issues dominated news headlines and news coverage.

[51]I refer mainly to the iPhone in this section because it was the most influential and iconic smartphone. The iPhone, along with the app industry it spawned, is arguably the main driver of the eventual popularity of smartphones worldwide. In 2019, the iPhone is a little under half the market share in the US, and around 20% of the market share globally.

Shortly after the launch of the iPhone, a whole industry of app developers sprouted up, creating new games, and other tools that would over the next decade deliver billions of hours of chatting, mindless swiping, emotionally charged reading, inattentive reading, and numerous other means for filling your head with content, data, or empty distractions from your immediate surroundings. All while making information, entertainment, and people more accessible, for less money, and more fun.

The annoying activities of waiting in line at the grocery store, doctor's office, or sitting on a crowded bus in traffic quickly became less of an annoying waste of time. These activities could actually become productive or even a little fun. The iPhone essentially gave you access to any information and almost anyone you wanted to engage with.

You could find an app to play or entertainment news to follow, or a friend to joke around with any time of day. When there was nothing physically around you that grabbed your interest, which started happening more often because our attention spans were perceptively shrinking, you could open an app and instantly be talking with friends or strangers across the world. Many of the potential downsides of fractured attention from having constant access to everything at all times were apparent early on but given very little serious consideration.[52]

What was completely obvious is that the iPhone made it easier for you to split your attention between multiple items in short increments. And one result was that this made it much more difficult to focus your full attention or deep levels of attention on a single item for longer stretches of time.

As iPhone users, we suddenly became more susceptible to becoming easily bored with being around a group of people that were

---

[52] In recent years people who work in technology have been more prone to speak directly about the potential dangers from the excessive Internet and smartphone use. Tristan Harris, encountered some of these issues while working at Google and testified at a US Senate hearing on June 25, 2019, https://www.youtube.com/watch?v=WQMuxNiYoz4.

Former V.P of user growth at Facebook, Chamath Palihapitiya made warnings of people being in a sense unconsciously programmed for certain behaviors, attitudes, and beliefs through the use of Social media. Discussion at Stanford Graduate School Dec 11, 2017, https://www.realclearpolitics.com/video/2017/12/11/fmr_facebook_exec _social_media_is_ripping_our_social_fabric_apart.html not constantly making us feel excited. If you had an iPhone, all you had to do was open your phone and find something not necessarily more exciting, but something that required less effort to remain engaged with. It felt rude, and it was rude, to open your phone amid a group of people, but everyone did it.

It became a constant competition to compare yourself with those you knew who stared at their phone more than you. It became a running joke about who would be "that person" to be staring at their phone throughout the party or some gathering.

As data plans improved and hard drive space on iPhones expanded over the years so did the graphics and usability. This all made people increasingly more attached to their iPhones. Whatever was on your smartphone screen became more engrossing as the social media and other apps developed improved methods to trigger our emotions. The aim of all the apps and data was pushing us to stay connected longer and leave a feeling in your brain to return for more when you left.

It was often through clever use of data and a series of personalized tricks used by app makers that made us feel that the app knew us better than most people in real life. Within a few years, you would see people constantly staring at their phones everywhere in public or private areas.

Between 2016–2019, I visited over 50 countries and observed the same behaviors everywhere. Whether I was in Brazil, Belgium, Ecuador, Sri Lanka, Slovenia, South Korea, Sweden, Ukraine, Ecuador, Turkey, Taiwan, or Ukraine people were staring at screens in the street, in coffee shops, on the trains, in clubs, concerts, waiting in line, or just sitting on a park bench surrounded by people. I saw it everywhere, all the time, people buried in their phones practically ignoring everyone and everything else around.

At the time, it was obvious to everyone that there were, and are, negative effects of staring at brightly glowing screens for hours a day. Beginning around 2012 I noticed lots of articles popping up about the downsides of smartphone usage. It's funny, that it was usually while you were staring at your glowing smartphone screen in a darkened room that you would read an article (usually you just read the headline and intro) of some recent study warning of the dangers of excessive staring smartphone screens.

People Forget That the iPhone Was Not an Immediate Success

Just before the launch of the iPhone in 2007, Clayton Christensen, a distinguished Harvard Business School professor, predicted that it would fail. Christensen wrote *The Innovators Dilemma* in 1997 and soon after became widely respected in business and investment circles. He is also credited with coining the term "Disruptive Technology," a phrase so overused by 2015 that it became synonymous with any successful or possibly successful Silicon Valley company.

It is surprising to think now, but when the iPhone came out, people were split on whether the iPhone would succeed or fail. Most people, older and younger, didn't grasp how big the iPhone would become.

Fortunately for Christensen, few recall or were ever aware of his early iPhone prediction. Christensen later explained[53] that his initial assessment of the iPhone was off because he missed the extent to which people would use iPhones as laptop replacements.

But he was not alone at all in how he saw the iPhone early on as skepticism was quite common. Like most people, Christensen had trouble finding where the iPhone would fit in with everything else going on with phones, technology, and the needs of people as it related to the Internet at the time. I remember learning about the iPhone before it came out and thinking that it seemed like a valiant effort by Apple.

Christensen's iPhone assessment had essentially no negative impact on his steadily burgeoning career, which continued to improve in the decade following the release of the iPhones. As the tech industry has grown to comprise a larger share of new jobs, wealth, and overall global economy Christensen's research and writings have become revered on Wall Street and Silicon Valley. Christensen's term "disruptive technology" continues to be used, and misused, with greater fre-

---

[53] The incorrect assessment of the iPhone along with Christensen's explanation can be found in a May 2012, New Yorker article https://www.newyorker.com/magazine/2012/05/14/when-giants-fail

quency on Wall Street, Silicon Valley, and in the global business and financial press since 2007.

In the early '90s, many Apple products had been a letdown as their products didn't live up to the hype. Apple had been very near shutting down permanently in the late '90s. In 2000, I was sitting in an introductory IT course when the instructor mentioned something about Apple computers and a student blurted out in a mocking tone, "What computers?" The instructor just smiled and said politely, "Hey now, let's be nice." This was the sentiment in the late '90s and early '00s, Apple was a failing company losing its relevance.

In the early '00s, iPod's popped up all over college campuses, coffee shops, and other cool places. In 2004, I remember driving through Long Beach California on the Interstate 405 freeway, seeing a cool iPod billboard, and thinking to myself, "I guess Apple will be around for a while after all." The iPod and other successes raised the public image of Apple.

But still, by 2007, despite seeing more Apple products around, most of the public was far from being convinced that it was a powerful tech company.

In March 2007, just a few months before the release of the iPhone, I visited my uncle in Washington, DC. He was probably the most knowledgeable Apple enthusiast I've ever known. My uncle explained how the iPhone would have a complete keyboard, and full Internet access, and other advantages over competing smartphones.

First, the full digital keyboard was a huge advantage. It made sending texts, emails, and other typing more easy and fun. I did know a few people that put off buying an iPhone because they thought their fingers were too small or too big. But for most, the keyboard was a big improvement on the existing alternatives.

Second, you could actually surf the web for real. Most phone models up to this point did not really let you access the full Internet. You could read short news or sports bits as I did on my Motorola V300 in 2004, but you couldn't actually search the web.

Third, the apps made the iPhone immensely more valuable. The apps became more valuable over time. In the first couple of years, many of the apps were useless because they were full of glitches. You downloaded an app that initially looked cool, but then ended up just deleting it a few weeks later after realizing you never used it. But the good apps stood out, and over time there were more and more good apps.

Some of the best early apps allowed you to play games with friends, check news feeds, stocks, and sports scores all in real-time. The real-time updates were a big change. You felt more connected constantly and it made the iPhone feel connected to your real life.

On a weeklong trip to Costa Rica in January 2009, a friend showed me a gaming app called *Field Runners*. The game was so much fun. We were stranded in the airport all day, and this game made the time pass easily. Soon after, I got an iPhone.

In May of 2009, I finally went to an Apple store in Scottsdale, Arizona and got an iPhone. Wanting to get the *Field Runners* gaming app drove this decision. Also, around this same time, I heard on NPR about new travel apps that were replacing travel books. I had just returned from two weeks in China where I carried around two heavy travel books, and a travel app sounded better.

A few months after I got the phone, I went on a kayaking trip with a friend outside Washington DC. I showed him the *Field Runners* app and he was immediately hooked. On the trip, every time we went to a restaurant or sat down for a few minutes, his face would light up as he asked, "Hey man, can I play that game again?"

A few days after the trip we spoke on the phone, and he told me "Hey, so I just bought an iPhone" and I responded, "did you really buy an iPhone just so you could play that *Field Runners* game?" Without any hesitation, he proudly confessed, "Dude, it was right at the front of my mind when I was buying it."

And so it was for so many people. One by one, people I knew found something that gave them a strong reason to buy an iPhone or some other smartphone. For a lot of us, it was discovering that first app that you really liked.

After 2009, I had multiple conversations with friends and colleagues about if or when they would buy an iPhone. By late 2009, my colleagues who had not purchased an iPhone started to justify not getting one if they didn't plan to get one soon. There was one iPhone app that everyone agreed had value, *Google Maps*.

Finding Yourself

Google Maps was the one app that everyone used. GPS systems had been in cars for years, but they were clunky to use so you primarily used them on longer trips. Also, GPS was only practical to use in your car because of the size of the device. With *Google Maps*, you could navigate while walking, cycling, and in all kinds of weird situations. It made your own city so much more accessible and almost totally eliminated the worry of getting lost when visiting a new city and country.

Those who were not around or not old enough to drive in the '90s are likely not capable of appreciating how awkward it was to drive to a new city or new area looking at some oversized driving atlas. Or how frustrating it was to get lost while deciphering poorly handwritten instructions. Mapping apps were such a relief, and literally opened up a world of opportunity for easier navigation.

In 2013, I was at a meeting in Washington, DC, and a guy who was around 50 years old told a story comparing life with and without *Google Maps*. 20 years earlier, he had been searching for a house one night on some windy old roads outside DC in northern Virginia. He ultimately gave up and headed home after searching in vain for two hours. He contrasted this with the experience of getting lost around the same area in 2013. With *Google Maps*, he found the house in about 20 minutes, saving around two hours.

Undoubtedly, there are millions, perhaps billions, of similar stories of getting lost then found through a mapping app. Speaking for myself, *Google Maps* has easily saved hundreds of hours in travels in many cities and countries throughout the world. Furthermore, it has opened up the possibility to go to places that I otherwise may not have found or tried to find in the first place, without *Google Maps*. In total, I estimate that *Google Maps* has saved billions of hours in time for people all over the world.

When I purchased my first iPhone in the middle of 2009 I had a monthly bill of around $40 for my cell phone. I justified the monthly bill increase to $80 by the *Google Maps* app. In the first months I kept track and easily saved hours each month.

The location feature on the iPhone also enabled a ton of uses and functions for apps. At first, many apps were predictable in using the location detection feature to find nearby restaurants or cheap gas stations.

But location detection would soon work its way into gaming, dating, shopping, and all sorts of other apps. It took a few years to improve app designs, build the algorithms, and also increase for people to adapt socially to using the location features that are now normal and essential.

The App Explosion

The explosion of apps following the iPhone launch in 2007 was crucial to the smartphone experience. Apple opened up to individual app developers who built apps that could be vetted and approved by Apple. Most of the early apps did suck and the apps churned out only improved gradually. However, the result of all these apps finding ways to draw our attention was people getting more hooked at staring at their smartphones.

As phones improved app developers found ways to more cleverly use data, pictures, video, and location content to make apps that were fun and addictive. Many of the successful and popular apps came up with smart ways of connecting people with other people in real-time. Since people more often saw the iPhone as an extension of their human experience, the apps that best allowed them to express themselves in fun, interesting, and real-time ways tended to stand out. This was a big step in merging the Internet world with the real world.

The timing of the app explosion was perfect. Between 2005–2010 there was an expansion of 3G data networks, high-speed broadband, and Wi-Fi in all kinds of public and private spaces. The most successful phones and apps seemed to be on the cutting edge of what data speeds and new improvements in smartphones.[54]

In hindsight, it is clear that Apple made the right call in opening up to individual developers. This allowed for faster innovation than if all apps were developed and vetted and filtered through a few large companies.

Very Angry Birds

In 2010, in the middle of a red-eye flight, I walked down the aisle toward the bathroom. Because it was a red-eye flight, everything was dark inside the plane, except for the area near the bathroom where I could see a colored glow emanating from a screen. I saw a flight attendant sitting down, focused, with rapt attention, and with a look of deep concentration on her face. I thought to myself, "Whatever she is doing, it must be very important." As I got closer, I got a better look and I saw that she was in the midst of an Angry Birds game on her iPad. She was in her 30s and didn't appear like a person who normally spent a lot of time playing computer games, but *Angry Birds* clicked.

Angry Birds was probably the first big gaming app to capture people's attention across the world. Beginning in late 2009 through 2011, everywhere you went you saw people playing Angry Birds. At lunch, waiting in line for coffee, and sitting hunched over in a cubicle at work, people launched these red, blue, and yellow birds at measured angles hoping to blow up those green pigs with annoying smiles.

Angry Birds came up in chats at work, conversations while traveling, and even part of a *Saturday Night Live* comedy sketche. People were hooked. I remember watching a Bloomberg interview with the Finnish founder of Rovio, which created the game and noticing how calm and nerdy he looked, even as his app dominated eyeballs everywhere.

This was at a time when most apps were duds, barely worth being downloaded. You just deleted them once you saw how they sucked. This made the breakaway success of *Angry Birds* stand out.

---

[54] This, of course, is an ongoing process in many parts of the world. Smartphones are just gradually becoming affordable for middle-class people in many developing countries, where Internet connections may be slow or unreliable, particularly outside the core urban areas.

CHAPTER SEVEN

NEW TECHNOLOGY
+ NEW VALUES
= NEW MUSIC

"Every generation hates the next trend in music they can't understand. We hate to give up those reins of our culture. To find our own music playing in elevators."

—Chuck Palahniuk, from the 2002 book, *Lullaby*

Beginning with the Baby Boomers in the '60s and on through Generation X in the '90s, rock music followed a more or less linear path. Most mainstream commercial music was derived in some way from the classic rock of The Beatles, The Beach Boys, Rolling Stones, Pink Floyd, The Doors, Bob Dylan, Jimi Hendrix, Led Zeppelin, Creedence Clearwater Revival, Queen, and many of their contemporaries. The biggest and most influential rock bands of the '90s: Nirvana, Pearl Jam, Red Hot Chili Peppers, Radiohead, Soundgarden, Green Day, Metallica, Stone Temple Pilots, Weezer, Blur, and Oasis all had very strong roots in rock music of the '60s.

'90s rock is distinguishable[55] in its heavier guitar sound, thicker distortion, and wider use of guitar effects than in the '60s.[56] But if you

---

[55] Commercial rock music of the '80s was highly commercialized, focused on the appearance of success and unabashedly self-serving. '90s alternative rock music had a lot in common with anti-establishment punk rock of the '70s and '80s. Whereas '90s rock was largely anti-establishment, anti-commercial, and in much more progressive on the political front.

[56] The guitar sound of the '90s was derived mostly from punk rock bands of the late '70s and '80s. Some bands that influenced the guitar sound were: The Sex Pistols, The Clash, The Stooges, The Ramones, and Black Sabbath.

look deeper at the song structures, melodies, vocal intonations, the influence of '60s music was a conscious choice.

From the '60s through the '90s as new technology developments and new instrument innovations became more affordable a change in music followed. If a new style was successful it would be imitated in excess. This would usually be followed by a backlash calling for more authentic, "real" music. A good example of this is disco, in the late '70s achieved mainstream success, but then quickly became a musical style that many rock fans loved to hate.[57,58]

From the '60s through the '90s technology significantly enhanced the musical recording process, instruments, and speaker sound quality. The technology also changed the formats that music was sold. Vinyl was replaced by cassettes, Cassettes were briefly replaced by 8-Tracks, then cassettes and 8-Tracks were replaced by CDs. But the fundamental business model was the same. The masses heard or saw music on the radio, or MTV and then went to the store to purchase the music and maybe went to see the music performed live.

The early '90s was a short-lived golden age for the big record labels. The switch to CD's in the late '80s and early '90s meant that the big labels which owned the rights to older music originally issued on vinyl could now reissue that music in CD format. The big labels made loads of money from re-releasing classic albums from The Beatles, The Doors, The Rolling Stones, and many more.

---

[57] On July 12, 1979, an event labeled "Disco Demolition Night" took place at Chicago's Comiskey Park with ~50,000 gathering at a Tigers vs. White Sox baseball playoff game to witness a crate full of disco records detonated on the field. The explosion was followed by rioting on the field. There was so much damage due to the incident that the White Sox forfeited the playoff game scheduled for the following night. Attendees who donated a disco record to be exploded were permitted for 98¢. Similar disco backlash events occurred in 1979 in Seattle and Portland.

[58] Similar backlashes to phases of technological advancement can be seen in other areas of culture and politics. Cultural trends, if big enough, will impact politics. Though it usually hits later. The reason is there is seldom an incentive for a politician to take a risk on a new cultural trend until it will certainly provide a net benefit to them.

In consequence, this left big records labels with plenty of cash to invest in a new generation of '90s music. '90s rock icons, Nirvana, Pearl Jam, Soundgarden, Stone Temple Pilots, Smashing Pumpkins all benefitted immensely from this arrangement.

There was a huge proliferation of rock bands in the '90s of all styles: alternative rock, indie rock, geek rock, math rock, space rock, noise rock, grunge, post-grunge, punk rock, punk-pop, punk-pop, riot grrrl, ska, Britpop, shoegaze, hardcore, post-hardcore, emo, metal, death metal, nu-metal, screamcore, industrial rock, drone, and many others which derived their influence in some way to the classic rock band setup. This was partly due to musical instruments becoming cheaper and more attainable for kids in the '80s.

Punk rock emerged and taught a whole generation in the '80s and '90s that you didn't need to play or sing well for people to enjoy your music. Chris Cornell, vocalist for Soundgarden in the '90s,[59] and acclaimed solo performer explained in a podcast interview that punk rock allowed him to envision himself making music because it broadened the definition of what music was and who could perform it.

The music industry expanded in the early '90s. But towards the end of the '90s, the music industry was in decline in part due to pressures from the Internet making free music more accessible. The decline was most pronounced in rock music genres. This meant that for many of the aforementioned rock variants, the competition was becoming more intense for a shrinking number of potential fans.

Another explanation for the decline of rock music could be as simple as the rock music sound and mindset didn't fit with the changing values and realities of the Internet era.

By the early '00s, there were fewer new rock artists that could hold a listener's attention. Most alternative rock radio stations that were founded in the '90s were replaying the same old hits from the '90s, with a smattering of a few new songs. Instead of a new style of

---

[59]WTF Podcast with Marc Maron, June 2014, http://www.wtfpod.com/podcast/repost-chris-cornell-from-june-2014

music coming along to replace alternative rock in commercial and cultural significance, rock entered a stasis.

During this time the music industry reoriented towards the recording and distribution of Rap, Hip Hop, R&B and similar variants. Building on mainstream traction starting in the late '70s Rap and Hip Hop artists exploded in popularity and commercial success in the '90s.[60] Artists like Jay-Z, N.W.A., Dr. Dre, Ice Cube, Snoop Dog, Tupac Pac Shakur, Lauryn Hill, Boyz 2 Men, Notorious B.I.G, Eminem, and many others were commercially and critically successful, along with having considerable influence in style, fashion, and culture.

One reason for the rapid success of Rap and Hip Hop at the time was the music and lyrics sounded fresh since the experiences and moods had not been heard in commercial music. They may have sounded especially fresh compared with listening to a '90s band doing another contrived copy of a rock riff or melody from a song of the '60s. Rock music may have sounded edgy, rebellious, and challenging to authority in the '60s, but something with even more edge was needed by the time the '90s rolled around.[61]

From the '50s through the '70s rock music revenue increased until plateauing in the '70s and '80s then increasing in the early '90s followed by big declines by the end of the decade. It would be reasonable to correlate revenue with general cultural influence. The early '90s was the last big wave of mainstream success for rock while Hip Hop, Rap, and R&B surged in commercial success.

---

[60] One thing often overlooked that record labels, and most companies, benefit when people buy products from fewer artists. This is due to focusing on marketing and promotional efforts on fewer artists. The basic economic theory asserts that limiting marginal costs (recording, promotions, etc.) a record label will profit far more from selling 10 million units for one artist than with selling 1 million units from 10 artists. Alternative rock by the late '90s was fragmented with way too many small and medium artists and not enough huge artists for the traditional labels to make money in the traditional way. There was also an anti-establishment attitude prevailing among many bands in the '90s, that if you were a success on commercial radio, you were a sellout and your music wasn't good.

[61] There may have also been some pent up demand for Rap and Hip Hop since large recording labels were slow or unwilling to produce and promote the music for years.

Nirvana cast a huge shadow over the rock music world in the early '90s. Nirvana helped the careers of bands with a similar sound while ending the careers of those with a different sound. Bands like Metallica and Guns N' Roses were drastically impacted by the success of Nirvana. Broadly speaking, Nirvana signaled an end to '80s hair bands. The autobiographies from two prominent '90s rock acts, Anthony Keidis, lead singer of Red Hot Chili Peppers, and Alex James, bass player for Blur, mentioned Nirvana more frequently and prominently than any other band. The success of Nirvana brought on the success of alternative rock, but music and culture were soon moving away from rock music.

There were structural issues at play as well. The Internet put the whole process of record labels producing and marketing music under serious strain because the music didn't need to be bought in a CD format. You could easily download music for free. Moreover, you could only download the songs you wanted, not get stuck paying $15 for only a couple good songs. As small record labels closed and big record labels consolidated in the mid-'90s so did radio stations consolidate or shut down.

The new economic realities brought about by the Internet put immense pressure on the artistic process. These pressures created a whole generation of creative types who placed greater emphasis on business savvy than originality and creative ideas. A frozen in time mentality in many creative sectors such as music took over. Creative energies and ideas were scrapped if they did not fit the new ideals of the post Internet world or appear to have immediate commercial viability.

Beyond music, other creative entertainment that involved any writing like TV, movies, and books from the late '90s and beyond was noticeably repetitive, bland, or lacking in the substance relative to what could have been produced. It felt like everything made was just an increasingly hollow echo of something that had been done or seen before.

I remember driving in my car in 2010 while listening to the radio in Phoenix Arizona, listening to an FM alternative rock station. Two songs came on that were both from the '90s, followed by Pearl Jam's ballad "Black" which was released in 1991. I thought back to hearing "Black" on the streets of northeastern Brazil in 2001. It seemed a bit old then, but not too out of place in Brazil's northeast region. Walking the streets you would regularly hear Roxette, ZZ Top and other '80s music in the street.

But this was 2010 in the United States, and I thought how weird it was to be hearing these songs on the radio. For over about 10 minutes everything that was played could have been heard 10–15 years earlier. The only difference was the commercials, which were new and annoying like always. It was as if almost nothing had happened in this genre of music for 15 years,[62] and this radio station was not an oldies station.[63]

Changing economics and demographics, and other factors likely contributed to this stasis in rock music. The impacts are certainly not confined to rock music, but it is perhaps a less studied and less understood area.

Rock music probably reached a point of cultural oversaturation somewhere in the '80s or '90s. Many rock acts of the '80s put fame and fortune at the forefront of their image. This obsession with success in the '80s turned around, making those who openly seeking fame to be labeled as posers, careerists, or wannabes in the '90s. Seeking fame and money in the '00s and beyond became 1 perfectly acceptable. But during the early '90s, the values were very different, and seeking fame and money implied you lacked artistic ability.

By the '90s, the rock 'n' roll model of playing in a band with your friends, working hard, getting a lucky break, and then hitting it big had been played out numerous times. Being a classic four-piece band

---

[62] *New York Times* writer Kurt Anderson addresses this theme of culture and style changing much less rapidly during the '90s and '00s compared with previous decades, supporting the idea that some stasis of culture and style were occurring in some sectors of entertainment. *Vanity Fair,* January 2012, https://www.vanityfair.com/style/2012/01/prisoners-of-style-201201

[63] In 2017, on at least one occasion I actually heard a radio station that referred to itself as an oldies station play '90s rock.

modeled after The Beatles, or a metal or punk rock band, was still an aspiration for many high school students, especially in suburban and rural high schools in the '90s, but less so in the '00s.

The classic rock 'n' roll story of success early on, followed by lots of partying, drugging, and had been played out so many times that it was a total cliché. Cliché or not, it didn't stop many people from trying out this well-worn path of rocking out, partying hard, getting addicted to some heavy drug (often heroin) or a slough of drugs, followed up by rehab and to focus on what "what really matters" or whatever the rock stars decided to repeat from their therapist.

By the late '90s, the US economy and job market had improved considerably, and many would-be rock stars found stable jobs and chose that overtaking a chance at becoming a rockstar. Financial stability and taking on grown-up responsibilities don't mix well with teenage angst and rebellion. Defying authority, which was a big part of the appeal of rock, was less appealing when jobs were easier to come by. Authority figures and bosses didn't seem so bad after all in an economy where bosses made more of an effort to keep employees from leaving.

Additionally, since fewer jobs were dangerous and dirty, some of the working class edges disappeared from music. There was a bigger trend of young people leaving historically industrial cities like Cleveland, St. Louis, Buffalo, Pittsburgh, and Detroit since much of the economic growth of the digital economy was not occurring in those cities.

Cleveland during the '50s was instrumental to the early formation of Rock 'N' Roll. Cleveland is home to the Rock 'N' Roll Hall of Fame and referred to as the birthplace of Rock 'n' Roll. Radio DJ Alan Freed sparked national trend during the '50s in promoting dances that would play "Rock 'n' Roll" at clubs for youth from all different classes and backgrounds, breaking down traditional class and racial barriers.

---

[64]In July 2015 I took a road trip from Washington, passing through Cleveland, Detroit, and Pittsburgh. These cities comprised the industrial core of the United States during the past century. They have experienced well-documented economic declines in recent decades. In Pittsburgh, I saw so many large parks with well-maintained green grass, but mostly empty. In Cleveland, I found easy parking on the 4th of July along the city

But by the late '90s, industrial cities[64] were losing lots of young people to cities growing tech and finance industries like San Francisco, New York, Seattle, and Boston. From the '90s to today a similar process of reallocating large numbers of educated workers to tech and finance-oriented cities has played out across the world. This has also contributed to gentrification, which is essentially younger people with money concentrating in cities, or areas of cities, that are most tied to the post-industrial economy.

Changing Family Values and Gender Norms

Gentrification and prolonging adolescence are notable characteristics of life for the generation born in the '80s. People placed a huge priority on pursuing passion projects, personal fulfillment, and maintaining a perception of excellence. The impacts on personal experience, society, politics, workplace life, cultural tastes, and micro and macroeconomic trends are remarkable. It may be years before there is some consensus on all the positive and negative outcomes. Living through it, it was hard not to observe the changes.

If you were in your 20s during the '00s, where you chose to live was less about finding a good neighborhood with quality school districts, and more about living close to a cool restaurant and bar scene, and being near people that think like you and living a similar lifestyle. Avoiding a long commute and being able to bike or walk to work became priorities for many; making living in the city was ideal.

People availed themselves of every online tool to search and find perfect roommates, housing, and neighborhoods that fit the life that they wanted to create. I remember responding to a Craigslist ad and getting interviewed by potential future roommates. They asked me about my schooling background and work. Then they asked me about

---

waterfront. In Detroit, minimal traffic in downtown and some revitalized areas amid decaying infrastructure. In these cities, the architecture tended to be older but still impressive and obviously built at the economic high points of those cities ~50–75 years prior. Nearly everyone I have told that I would visit those cities thought I was crazy, but I found it to be a refreshing look at some US cities that had some great history.

my sleeping and social patterns. They then inquired about my dietary and exercise habits. As I spoke it was as if they were just looking for someone exactly like them, allowing very little wiggle room for someone different. We did watch a few of the same Netflix shows, so we discussed that briefly, but I wasn't surprised when I didn't make the final cut for this audition for a roommate.

Increased disposable income meant more money spent on high-end toys, vacation deals with groups of singles or just yourself. Loads of new websites offered flight deals or flash sales of designer clothing and high-end gadgets. People would stare at all these shopping options while at work or in class every day. People did occasionally buy something, but more often they just stared at the deals, sent them to friends, and let your mind fantasize about it from your computer at your desk.

Those who grew up in the '80s were the first generation to grow up in a situation where birth control was widely reliable, accessible, and socially acceptable. It was mass-marketed, low-price, and available in most areas of the United States, and much of the world as well. Many public schools gave detailed descriptions of the different birth control options.

Medical research constantly claimed in commercials and other advertising there were many health benefits from birth control use. These ads became so frequent that one female friend of mine once joked how "birth control advertising is basically saying 'do you have acne? Try birth control pills! Need to lose weight? Birth control pills will fix that! Are you depressed? Before we try anything else, let's try birth control pills! That's the answer!'"

Public schools also had many programs teaching about the risks of an array of Sexually Transmitted Diseases (STDs). The big STD during the '80s and '90s was AIDS. I cannot recall exactly how many times we were taught about AIDS from 1st grade through the end of high school, but it was a lot. In total, during 5th grade, 6th grade, 8th grade, and 9th grade there were many hours devoted to instruction on AIDS education and prevention. For those born in the '80s, sex was portrayed as being dangerous, scary, and with lots of negative consequences.

That view persisted in the minds of many kids for much of the '90s and beyond.

Meanwhile, the idea of marriage became a lot less cool. Teachers, parents, and the stories in the news were all about people following their dreams and finding personal fulfillment. Following your dreams was a very individual experience. It was YOUR DREAM that YOU NEED TO ACCOMPLISH or else your life will be unfulfilling, and without value or relevance.

I remember in 1999 sitting in an English writing course Bellevue Community College,[65] and the instructor, who was female and around 50 years old, complained frequently about a former student she had. She would say how "this student didn't care much about improving her writing since she was so focused on just passing the class so she could go off, get married and have kids". The goal of having a family was looked down on as being "less fulfilling" for women and for men as well.

Whether it was teaching gorillas sign language in Africa, exploring and preserving the Amazon rainforest, climbing the seven summits on seven continents, there was always something bigger and larger to accomplish out in the world somewhere. And you had to go out and find it or else your life would have less meaning. Moreover, the idea that you could have it all, pursuing all your dreams, a lucrative career, and still have plenty of time for family was widely accepted at face value by the generation born in the '80s.

Many didn't consider, or were encouraged not to consider, economic limitations or the potential costs of following your passion.[66] Many also assumed there would be little to no negative impacts on your social life from following dreams or a demanding professional

---

[65] I took classes at a Community College while in high school to earn college credits. The program was called Running Start and targeted students who were anxious to get on with college life. I loved the program and so did the 500 students who also participated.
[66] PBS NewsHour video clip examines how many middle-class people have difficulty saving and covering expenses for emergencies when they are in a career that cannot pay for their lifestyle. Interviewer Judy Woodruff states how many are told "so many young people today are told find your passion and follow it" but unaware of the limiting circumstances this could put you in. June 2016 https://www.youtube.com/watch?v=tamC-M8TxtY

life, but that is simply not true. It was as if everyone had these high expectations of everyone else because they believed it was possible and not believing it was possible was just inherently wrong.

In the academic school year of 1981–1982, the total bachelor's degrees earned by women exceeded[67] those earned by men. This trend has continued, and though it does vary by discipline, university, and geographical location, women have earned roughly 57% of all bachelor's degrees annually awarded since.

Those born in the '80s are the first to grow up in a world in which both men and women graduated from college at near-equal rates. Additionally, it's the first generation where both men and women who worked hard in attaining their bachelor's degrees and wanted to use their acquired skills could realistically envision doing so.

Those born in the '80s and later entered the workforce in the '90s or '00s have only known a world where women attain college degrees at equal, or greater, rates than men. Furthermore, the expectation or potential to enter the professional work world is vastly greater than the options available to those born in the '60s, '70s or earlier.

It is such a dramatic shift in the mindset that it is difficult for younger generations to fully comprehend. My 4th-grade teacher, who entered the workforce in the '60s, explained that essentially the only career options possible for women at that time were nurse, flight attendant, and school teacher. But for both men and women born in the '80s, for the most part, only knew a world with relatively few occupations entirely cutoff. It was also more acceptable for men to become nurses, flight attendants, and school teachers than it had previously been.

In 2007, I entered the corporate world along with many others from the generation born in the '80s. The Internet and the knowledge economy made it more possible to diminish the barriers for women

---

[67]According to the National Center for Educational Statistics, in 2016–2017, women had earned 57% of all bachelor's degrees, for the 18th consecutive year. https://www.cnsnews .com/news/article/terence-p-jeffrey/women-earn-57-us-bachelors-degrees-18th -straight-year

born in the '80s to enter many areas of the workforce that were not possible just years earlier. At the companies I worked for this was normal, but this didn't appear to be the same across all industries and depended a lot on the company, department, or manager.

For the entry-level position I had, strategic forecast analyst at US Airways, it appeared that men and women had a nearly even chance of getting hired. Most people in the Revenue Management department were men, but men were more interested in those jobs and applied for those jobs more often. Among the women who were hired and remained with the company, many became managers. The time I worked there, between 2007–2011, both managers were women.

I remember one time speaking with a co-worker who ran a professional women's association, a networking group for women. She said in essence "I really don't feel like my career opportunities are limited here as a woman. No place is perfect, but I think that if I want to pursue an opportunity it won't be closed off to me as a woman."

This was not the reality in many workplaces and the situation varied greatly depending on the company, city, region, state, or country of the world. But, most agreed that equality of opportunity had increased significantly compared with my parents' generation.

Frozen in a Singles Mindset and Prolonging the College Social Experience

Around this time, many entry-level jobs requiring a bachelors degree went like this: constant instant messaging between colleagues at work and friends at other jobs, getting coffee daily, weekly happy hours, forming cliques to stay notified of office snacks and workplace gossip, and occasional office pranks in between some sterile meetings, researching for a better job, and about half the time spent on the boring tasks of your job for which you were paid.

This all meant that it felt like an extension of the college social experience. But now you made money and had a bit more responsibility. Both men and women who were college graduates entered the workforce in roughly equal numbers. And most put a priority on progressing their career, but having fun times with co-workers was also a priority.

Many young college graduates in large cities spent much of their 20s focused on themselves and building their careers. If people did choose to have kids, it was often later in their storyline than in previous generations. Accordingly, there was a sharp growth of the pregnancy and fertilization industry with doctors and specialists using pricey equipment to assist a generation of older and more professionally experienced people produce children in their late 30s, 40s and beyond.

I knew several people who used such services. They had worked hard and been very successful professionally, so paying the high annual fees was not an issue. High fees were a perfectly viable option to ensure a high probability of success in having multiple children. I had some roommates in DC who grew up in the west of the United States saying they "were reminded they were living on the East Coast" when they saw a billboard for fertilization services with a tagline "so you can have a family when the time is right." By 2017 there were numerous startups and news articles promoting fertilization services.

At many companies incentives were in place for both men and women to devote more and more time on the job and investing more of their life energy into their careers. This did fit with the lifestyle preferences and professional goals of many, at least as they perceived them at the time.

But an interesting change occurred in the attitudes towards the work environment. Just as the average number of hours people spent at work increased there was an increasing focus on finding a work-life balance. Some of the companies that were the most visible in promoting a balance of being productive and also ensuring it provides deeper fulfillment in life were startups and prominent tech companies. Flexibility with work hours, freedom to pursue personal projects, tolerance for social life interfering with work.

Single lifestyles had been celebrated long before the '90s. But there was a noticeable change in the early '90s in how TV shows put more emphasis on the upside and less emphasis on the downside of single life. As portrayed in TV shows like *Friends*, *How I Met Your Mother*, and *Sex in the City*, single life was a fun loaded stream of endless happy hours, hanging out in cool coffee shops, fancy getaways, and exciting hookups.

Watching those shows convinced many people that life as a single could be as fun or more fun than college. In many ways it was more fun. You usually had greater independence, higher disposable income, and, especially in larger cities, there were many people at work in the same boat. That meant lots of parties, professional networking, meetups, and fun getaway trips to the Carribean or Mexico with people on the same track. This social ecosystem made it easy to avoid maturing socially.

By 2008, you could stream most TV and music at fast speeds throughout most of the United States. Hulu, Netflix, Amazon, all got into the streaming business and people followed. If you were in your 20s, it was normal to listen to the same music and watch the same TV and movies that you watched in high school and college. You could feed yourself on a steadily streamed diet of nostalgia, and many did this in excess, preventing new thoughts or maturity.

Your income increased, your job skills improved, but your mindset and sense of culture often didn't, because you could just consume the same entertainment through the Internet for years. We kept moving along, aging without noticing, listening to the same music, watching the same TV shows, repeating the same social experience for years.

Most people did choose to marry or have long-term relationships. But there was a significant and increasingly large share of people that were essentially in a perma-single status. I knew several guys who married in their mid-20s, divorced around 30, and then remained single for years, not showing much interest in marrying again.

Larger cities seemed to continually attract youth and embrace independence and personal freedom. I would see friends, both men and women, make occasional posts on social media something about the loneliness they felt from not having a romantic partner or frustration with the dating situation. Most guys talked about how they felt about being single infrequently, but when they did open up there was plenty of pain and disillusionment with the lack of fulfillment.

For much of the '90s, '00s, and beyond there was a lot of societal emphasis on prolonging singleness for as long as possible. Men and women seemed to be affected equally, though in different ways and with different responses.

I remember meeting a female friend in Washington DC in 2013, who observed, "I am 34, but my life has barely changed since I was 24." And when she said that, it was obviously an unpleasant thought if one stopped to think about it, but it wasn't uncommon and didn't seem at all out of place.

For many in this generation, it was so easy to let your mind come under the allusion that little had changed since your time as a recent college graduate. For those alive in the '90s, '00s, and '10s, the Internet contributed to prolonging adolescence, this was especially acute for those born in the '80s and '90s.

CHAPTER EIGHT

FUTURE WORK

It is now much less about finding the right company
and more about being found by the right company.

"80% of success in life is showing up"[68] Most people born in the '80s and earlier are very familiar with this quote. But does this advice still hold true?

In the book, *The World of Yesterday*, renowned Austrian author of his day, Stefan Zweig, describes a visit to New York City in 1907. It was his first visit to the United States, and he spoke almost no English. Observing that the New York City of 1907 had few tourist attractions he decided it would be more interesting to walk around the city and act as if he were a new immigrant searching for a job to test the claim of America being the "land of opportunity."

For three days, and with no prior job contacts, Zweig walked around Manhattan inquiring for work. Each day he secured offers for several jobs that would pay enough to cover rent of a private apartment, food, transportation, and also set aside money for saving. The jobs didn't require specialized skills, a referral, or even to speak English, just showing up and working was all that was required.

Those born in the '80s grew up at the tail end of the Industrial era. My first experiences in job-hunting in the late '90s were more

---

[68]Attributed to Woody Allen during a 1977 interview following the release of the movie *Annie Hall*.

similar to what Zweig encountered in New York in 1907, in the middle of the Industrial Era than what job searching has become today.

For much of the '90s, getting a job was often about showing up and proving you could do the job. There was much less of endless emailing faceless organizations, filling out job questionnaires or quizzes, or making it through several interviewers and other obstacles courtesy of a Human Resources (HR) Department.

Today in New York City, and most large cities, just showing up and finding a job that can pay enough to cover the expenses that Zweig in 1907 found he could cover (rent an apartment, food expenses, transportation, and saving) is all but impossible without prior experience and/or specialized skills. Securing such a job often requires skills in high demand, normally acquired with years of expensive education, leveraging the right connections, and appropriate social skills, which vary greatly for each office and company subculture. Initiative and showing up have much less to do with who gets and keeps the job.

In 1998, I got my first part-time job at the *Seattle Times*.[69] Getting this job was more about taking the initiative than any skills that I possessed. Finding job ads in the newspaper and calling them up was how a lot of people found jobs. Qualifications and prior experience were less essential than a willingness to work and learn. Initial face-to-face interactions mattered a lot.

Much of the job advice that I remember hearing from older generations was: "put yourself in the right place at the right time" or "take the initiative and get the job." At the time, I listened to many stories from the careers of older people. Older people often shared stories about finding a job that went like this: "I walked over to the store, told them I was interested in a job, and they looked at me, said they didn't know me, but they would give me till the end of the week to show if I could do the job."

---

[69] I was 16 and still in high school. My first job requiring a Bachelor's degree was in 2007 for US Airways in Phoenix Arizona.

There were so many TV shows from the '70s or '80s where a man or woman walking down a generic main street comes across a help wanted sign. They walk in the store, take down the Help Wanted sign, and have the job by the next scene. The '90s still resembled this process, but you were looking at ads and calling by phone and then showing up.

Before, people were more limited in what jobs they could encounter from walking around looking for "Help Wanted" signs, looking in the paper, or talking to friends. Furthermore, job growth has been focused in areas requiring highly technical or specialized skills. Many of the lower-skilled and non-specialized jobs available are far more competitive and do not provide the standard of living as in previous points in US history.

The Internet made it a lot easier for people to find jobs. Returning to the quote at the beginning of the chapter: "80% of success in life is showing up." You never really hear this quote anymore and most people born after the early 90s are not familiar with it. The reason for this is obvious.

But the bigger change was how it became far easier for companies to find people with the right skill set. It became much less important for you to find the right company because the Internet made it so much easier for companies to find the right person.

The Internet did make it easier for applicants to flood company inboxes and HR systems with resumes and job applications. But do companies care? Not really, because the companies can now more easily focus their efforts on finding the right people, and this is a more effective use of time than sifting through a thousand resumes or answering hundreds of phone calls. So companies really don't care who "shows up" at their door or virtually "shows up" in their inbox. Companies can search and find who they need. Showing up doesn't really make their job easier.

If your skills line up with what a recruiter is looking for you can skip that whole annoying application and interviewing process. The Internet has made it much easier for companies to find talent or poach talent from competitors. Companies are often quite direct about the transactional and impermanence of their employment, even for professionally skilled jobs for people with bachelors and graduate degrees.

Much has been said about younger people being less loyal to companies. But relatively little has been said about the Internet facilitating less commitment to their employees. Thus, many companies have reduced or eliminated training programs and instead lean more heavily on HR to find replacements with all the skills they need.

This has many implications for the future of work. For one, finding an individual or team of freelancers to complete a special project is far easier now. Companies are using this to hire for short-term jobs or projects instead of taking on full-time staff. The future of work may involve companies hiring more freelancer managers who manage no permanent employees, whose job is to go out and assemble teams to accomplish specific tasks.

These changes are often very positive since they are more efficient. However, one downside is that it may remove the incentives for employees to contribute their best ideas to the future of the company. Companies viewing employees merely as readily replaceable skillsets cause employees to adapt and often contribute less. Moreover, there may be social consequences as well, causing people to have fewer strong social connections and greater social isolation.

In a literal sense "showing up" matters less as working from home and remote work options have become more common. I have walked through multiple offices of large corporations and big startups at 10 am on a Wednesday and found it virtually empty. On multiple occasions, I just saw some chatting interns, scattered mid-level employees, and several high-level staff in offices.

In 2013, Yahoo ordered remote workers to return to the office.[70] This decision apparently didn't improve Yahoo's competitive or financial

---

[70] Yahoo! recalling people working from home to the office was big news at the time and widely discussed in the US media for its impact on work-life balance and expectations: February 25, 2013, New York Times, https://www.nytimes.com/2013/02/26/technology/yahoo-orders-home-workers-back-to-the-office.html

performance because it floundered afterward and until being formally acquired by Verizon a few years later.

Working from home does expose a generational divide. I have
heard people older than me describe working from home as nice for a
day or two, but makes them go crazy if they work isolated at home for an
extended period. Contrasting this many people my age or younger who
work from home and they almost all love it. As it becomes more common
and socially accepted, society will adapt and it will be more interesting.

In other words, as with most social changes brought about by the
Internet, the more people do something, it becomes more normalized
and enjoyable for a wider range of people. Working from home may
have initially only appealed to a small portion of people who benefit
from being outside an office. Many people are accustomed to socializing with their work colleagues or at least not being alone all day. But as
more and more people work remotely or work from home, the tools
available to stay socially connected have improved thus reducing the
effects of social isolation caused by working from home.

Another reality that has occurred in correlation but not necessarily caused by the Internet economy is the prevalence of company
founders and executive teams over-representing Ivy League schools.
There are multiple reasons for this, but it mostly comes down to the
fastest legal way to build wealth in the United States is being an owner
or major stockholder of a successful company.

Most of the leading investment banks have executive teams and
top employees who went to Harvard, Yale, Stanford, and other elite
universities. People typically invest in people they know and trust and
this is usually in companies with founders who went to those same
Universities. Alumni connections also facilitate angel investment and
venture capital investment, which is pivotal to the success of tech
companies. These investments, in turn, become an essential factor in
which companies are the best-funded, have the most success, and
ultimately become the most successful.

If you work for a company with an executive team that went to
elite universities, the chances to move very far up the ladder are probably limited unless you went to one of the same schools. On the other

hand, if you work for a company with executives that didn't go to elite universities, you are less likely to have been enjoying the benefits of venture capital and other financial options which have been key drivers of growth in the US economy in the past couple decades.

There used to be stories of CEO's at McDonald's beginning as a cashier, or Bank executives who started out the in the mailroom. But those stories are mostly gone now and there are essentially no high-level employees who spend their entire careers at a single company. Moving up the ranks is just not realistic in many of the largest companies today.

This environment is much less geared towards those who take initiative and expose themselves to risks. It favors those who cultivate a network long in advance, often based on family socio-economic status, geographic position, and educational opportunities early in life, which most kids have little to no control over. Careful guidance from parents, teachers, and professional mentors beginning in early in life has replaced initiative and drive to succeed.

In conclusion, opportunities are plentiful in the United States, but it has benefitted people with certain skillsets far more than others. It is often discussed how it is much easier to find and apply for jobs, but what it is less often discussed is how much companies have benefitted from making it easier to find the people they want. Showing up and taking initiative is much less important. Being easily found and having the skills that people want to find matters far more.

Working Apps—The Sharing Economy

For most of 2012, I lived in Boston near the Roxbury Crossing metro, and later in Brookline. Since I had no car, I used the T-line metro rail system for commuting to work and getting around Boston. Most of the core areas of Boston are quite accessible by public transit, but this is much less the case outside these main areas.

To get around, I rented a car a few times, borrowed my roommates' car occasionally, and sometimes a friend would offer me a ride. There is a unique sense of community in Boston, easier to experience than explain. People reach out and help each other in the time of need.

Maybe this is because Boston, with such a high density of universities, retains such a strong atmosphere of a college town.[71]

One evening I was riding in my friend Jonathan's car along Mass Avenue and I remember seeing multiple groups of people standing along the curb of the sidewalk waiting for a taxi. As a joke, I blurted out, "Hey, if they are going the same way, maybe we could pick up a few people and drop them off wherever they are going. $20 is $20." It was just a joke, so we laughed.

But, there was something in the air in 2012, because picking up strangers in your car didn't seem as unacceptable anymore. This is in part because smartphones had enabled a comfort with strangers that few anticipated. The popularity of Facebook and other social media apps facilitated quick vetting of people, and this was a game-changer.

By this point, Uber (started 2009), Lyft (started 2012), and Airbnb (started 2008) had been around for a few years but they were not yet well known or mainstream.

By 2012 the zeitgeist was ready for something like ridesharing with strangers. Granted, this was more predominately among younger people and people using smartphones for most aspects of their life, but it soon spread to others. The distance people felt in their heads with strangers had dissipated with the rise of social media.

Who we defined as a "stranger" became less clear as the Internet was more trusted and essential to each facet of our lives. Few anticipated that soon after smartphones became popular in 2008 people would become more comfortable with "strangers" than people had been in decades, but that is what happened. Soon, large numbers of people were using apps like Uber and Airbnb get into a car or a house of someone they had never met, in a way that had been inconceivable a few years prior.

People trusted their smartphones and how the Internet could verify information on people. You could see a person's name, picture,

---

[71] An example of this community friendliness occurred after the tragic 2013 Boston Marathon bombing. There were numerous reports of Bostonians opening their homes to support runners, visitors affected by the attack. https://www.theatlantic.com/national /archive/2013/04/photos-stories-kindness-boston-marathon-bombing/316237/

and you could message or call that person, and contact the support team on the app with problems. The review system was absolutely essential to making this system work. People trusted the apps to remove bad actors and also encourage good behavior through the review system. If someone did something wrong, it would be hard for them to get away it.

At some point between 2007–2018, we as a society passed a major inflection point where the majority of people, and the vast majority of younger people, felt comfortable with meeting and extending trust to someone they met through an online app.

In 2009, I had a roommate named Shawn. He described his first interactions with his then-fiancé: "We didn't really know each other, we had maybe talked briefly once or twice. But we had a few mutual friends and so I friended her on Facebook. Then once we started chatting through Facebook. She later told me that once we started chatting on Facebook is when she started to like me."

After dating for a few months they were engaged. However, the engagement ended a few weeks into the engagement period. They didn't remain Facebook friends after the breakup. Even though it ended badly, this story was one of many I heard from friends and acquaintances who around this time found it more comfortable communicating through social media or some other form of Internet communication than in person. They liked that digital layer of separation.

By around 2015, many people I knew actually found it easier to trust someone they met online through social media than a person they just met on the street, at least initially. One study showed this change. In 2012, more teens (49%) preferred talking in person than texting or online messaging (42%), but by 2018 fewer teens preferred chatting in person (32%) than texting or chatting online (35%).[72] One study in 2015, found that over half of teens had made multiple friends online.[73]

---

[72] Study performed by Common Sense Media, cited in Insider.com September 12, 2018. https://www.insider.com/study-teens-would-rather-text-with-friends-than-hang-out-in-real-life-2018-9

This was a landmark genertion change in mindset. During the early years of the Internet, people you met on the Internet were generally imagined as this unknown, unverifiable, group of potentially dangerous people. It was hard to verify who people were since most people lived much less of their life online than they do now.

During the '90s and early '00s, most people had mental barriers and distinctions between people you knew in real life and could trust and the "strangers" in the online world that you mostly could not trust. But there was a mainstreaming effect, and as more people used the Internet for all kinds of things, the more normal it became. By 2018, many of those barriers had melted away.

People born in the '80s can probably remember growing up and hearing numerous warnings at school of the dangers of taking rides with strangers. "Never get into a car to take a ride with someone you don't know." These warnings were driven by reactions to some high profile child abductions in the '70s and '80s that drew national media attention to the issue of child abduction.

Also, as the Internet became more popular in the '90s, there was loads of fear-mongering against all the potential bad people on the Internet. Some of this was valid, there was, and still are, plenty of scams, false information, and predatory people using the Internet. The negative stigma did stick for many in the first generation. But this negative stigma appears to have not been as strong for those born after the early '90s.

Perhaps the most unique, distinguishable, and interesting feature in the world is the human face. A critical component to making people trust the Internet more was easier access to quality digital photography allowing people to put their face online. With familiar faces, the Internet felt more personable and trustable.

Facebook, more than any other company was responsible for making people feel more comfortable with putting their faces online. For most kids in High School or College after 2008, having a Facebook profile was an absolute social necessity.

---

[73] Pew Research Study, cited in *The Guardian*, August 6, 2015. https://www.pewinternet.org/2015/08/06/teens-technology-and-friendships/

Sharing economy apps like Airbnb and Uber to a large extent piggybacked on the social trust advanced by Facebook. Within a few years, it became very normal to extend a great deal of trust to people met through the Internet. A whole new level of work and economic activity was thus enabled.

CHAPTER NINE

GENERATIONAL RIFTS EMERGE

One afternoon in early 1997, my dad quoted an article in *Popular Science* magazine to my brother and myself which read: "The Internet is slow, boring, and largely a waste of your time." The emphasis my Dad put on "sssslooowww" and "booorrring" made his opinion clear. But, I then picked up the magazine and read the next sentence, which continued on, "But you have to try it."

At the time, I was like a lot of kids around my age, I used the Internet and thought it was cool. My dad was born in 1946, the first year of the baby boom, he was like most boomers of the time, skeptical about the Internet thing.

But sure enough, in the next few months, my dad was like a lot of people in his generation, gradually spending more time online as they saw more and more things that were relevant to them. As he started to use the Internet more, he justified it by saying: "it's like reading a magazine."

Most Baby Boomers did eventually embrace the Internet, but adoption was slow. Most had their first contact with the Internet in the mid-90s when they were in their '40s or early '50s. Many of the early architects and pioneers of the Internet were actually born just before or during the Baby Boom period.[74] However most of the early adopters, both consumers and producers of the Internet were much younger,

---

[74] Tim Berners Lee, born in 1955, built what became known as the World Wide Web. John Perry Barlow, born in 1947, was a songwriter for the "Grateful Dead" and influential in the early culture of the Internet and maintaining freedoms to enable anyone to find

and consequently, a lot of the content was oriented towards teenagers and college students. Initially, there were few social or professional incentives for Boomers to be online.

In these years '97–'98, the Internet was so slow compared with high-speed broadband today. And with slow speeds, one frustration problem was clicking on links that would then take minutes to open up. The trouble was, it was impossible to predict which links would take only seconds, and which would clog up your screen for minutes.

The computer screen froze up all the time. This could be a frustrating dilemma in particular when you only clicked on a link out of passing curiosity, and then you would sit there waiting and wondering what went wrong. One time I remember my Dad yelling out, "Sorry! I didn't mean to click it, go back!" while tapping his fingers hard on the table and clicking in vain. Everyone experienced this repeatedly.

Around this time, there was a bizarre emergence of chain emails. Chain emails were sent and passed around to thousands of people across the world. They shared all kinds feel-good positive stories, embellished health cure claims, made calls to action for humanitarian causes, or vaguely promised good things if you passed along the email. The power of interconnection and networking effect of the Internet was quickly apparent. I heard multiple people claim they received chain emails that had also been received independently by friends all over the world.

There was a proliferation of celebrity gossip, dramatically exaggerated news stories, sensational rumors, and weird rumors that sounded like news that showed up in emails and on websites. These were some of the first obvious signs of what could be called the ugly underbelly of the Internet. The Internet made a good home for all kinds of tantalizing and extravagant claims or information that couldn't make it past a mainstream media or entertainment editing.

---

information about anything. Vint Cerf, born in 1943, and Robert Kahn, born in 1938, preceded the Baby Boomer generation and are the most important designers of the protocols that are the foundation of Internet infrastructure.

The information deluge was certainly disorientating, but it did provide a glimpse of what information attracts attention when unfiltered by traditional media outlets.[75] The power the media held over the distribution and consumption of information was challenged for a while in this early period. But eventually traditional media moved their content into online platforms and the Internet became more welcoming to the mainstream audiences and older generations. Over the next few years the Boomers, Generation X, and early Millennials (those born in the '80s) were all using the Internet in large numbers.

Events Define Generations

The Internet has had a greater impact on the: social behavior, learning process, relationship habits, attention spans, culture, attitudes, world perspective, religious belief, political preference, physical posture, and trust towards institutions of government and media than any other developent since the end of World War II. In other words, and the Internet has made the greatest impact on the generations growing up with it than any other event or technology since the conditions imposed on the boomers following World War II.

The Boomers were largely defined by the strong position of the US following WWII and subsequent Cold War policies. The post-war economic, cultural, and political realities heavily influenced the Boomer's values and conception of social life and these attitudes, values, and beliefs were a break from the attitudes, values, and perspectives of previous generations.

As the Internet became more popular a rift emerged between those for whom the Internet was an important and pivotal part of their life and those for whom this was less true. The division was more

---

[75] In a 1996 interview David Foster Wallace stated that a key challenge of the Internet would be effectively managing the massive and uncontrolled flow of information made through the openness of the Internet. Unmanaged information could be very unappealing if not organized in a way to make it comprehensible and appealing. These comments are in the 2010 book *Although Of Course You End Up Becoming Yourself: A Road Trip with David Foster Wallace*, by David Lipsky.

or less along generational lines, but not entirely so. The generational divide became more pronounced over time. The age with which you started regularly using the Internet seemed to be a big factor. I have met people that didn't use the Internet until after High School, despite most of their friends using it, the difference in social habits and attention span is immediately noticeable.

From the Boomers through Generation X and to the Millenials, it could be said that the cultural norms, ethical values, and expectations have continued more or less along the same continuum of norms, values, and expectations. People consumed books, music, and other media in the same way and following similar patterns.

Those who grew up after the early '90s[76] with the Internet being a part of their entire life, represent a break from these values. Whether consciously acknowledged or not are essentially pursuing a whole set of ethical values, social habits, expectations of others, relationship with institutions, permanency of decisions, access to information, and many others.

However, those born in the '90s do have one feature in common with the Boomers. They were both born at the cusp of a big change in reality. Being born at the dawn of a new era comes with some big advantages and disadvantages. On the one hand, you are perhaps best positioned to see opportunities when there is the biggest reward for seeing such advantages. On the other hand, you suffer the consequences of not knowing what mistakes to avoid and testing out the technologies before the risks are better understood.

For example, recreational drug use and driving cars were generally more dangerous in the '60s and '70s due to inferior safety methods, knowledge of the chemicals being more limited, and less quality

---

[76]This first generation born in the post Internet era is often referred to as Generation Z. Since other names and labels are in common use to define the cohort born after the early '90s, I refer to this group as the generation born after the mid-'90s. In this book, I avoid excessive use of generational where possible since I believe focusing on these labels puts more attention on the more superficial aspects and distract from understanding the deeper distinguishing features.

control. In the '90s and '00s, overuse of prescription medications and harm from the excessive use of the Internet posed a bigger threat to youth and adults. This is in part because Internet websites and services and prescription drugs were intelligently and aggressively marketed to convince people that using them was the solution to a variety of problems. The physical, mental, and social downsides of the excessive Internet or prescription drug use were not properly assessed.

Boomers achieved and maintained outsized political power due to the largest single demographic unit. Whether driving issues through protest or demonstration during the Vietnam era or in holding public office they were able to hold and maintain economic advantages and social opportunities for their generation. With these benefits, they were able to nudge out those born in smaller sized generations born a few years earlier or later.[77]

Literary and culture critic Stephen Metcalf commented that the Boomers were the first generation that succeeded in demanding that movies, TV, entertainment and other media speak to them on their terms and in their manner of speech and vernacular.[78] The same cannot be said about Gen X or the Millenials, but the present Internet Generation is coming close in influence.

In 2012, those born after 1990 were entering the workplace in large numbers. At this time I noticed a lot more articles in Bloomberg, Wall Street Journal, and other media discussing/applauding/complaining/freaking out/ about dealing with the different values and mindsets of the wave of Millennials. By 2015, the term millennial had become strongly associated with being young, smart, and cool and people were proud to be associated with it.

Living through it, anyone could see the rifts separating the generally younger people that understood and liked the Internet, and the generally older people who saw less relevance or meaning found on

---

[77] An excellent case in point was mentioned at the outset of this book, the three presidents all elected from the first year of the Baby Boom; Clinton, Bush, Trump. The generation born in the early '90s may be able to do the same.

[78] Stephen Metcalf, made this comment on an episode of the Slate Culture Gabfest podcast.

the Internet. People talked about this all the time. In 2017, I met a new college professor who was 27 and taught at small liberal arts college near Philadelphia comment:

> "These kids are only a few years younger than me, but they have used the Internet their whole lives and they use it for everything. Even though I am only a few years older I actually feel very far apart from them."

It is interesting to note the rise in attention on differences between generations in the United States in recent years. Around 2013, I noticed how people I knew from other countries, such as China, could effortlessly discuss distinct challenges and opportunities affecting the different generations. In recent years there has been a sharp increase in the United States in the attention given to generations and generational change.[79]

Anyone living in the United States in recent years can recall many instances of seeing news articles addressing generational differences, research blaming Boomers for employment stagnation, social media posts starting out "as a millennial ... " followed by some statement of generational perspective, or discussions with friends and co-workers stating "I'm from a different time ... " and explaining how things were done differently.

In summary, you can draw a line connecting the social attitudes, beliefs, and values of the Boomers, through Generation X and to the early Millenials. But for those born in the early '90s and beyond there is a break with this pattern of connected values. This is the most significant generational break at least since the Boomers and with its many implications is likely to continue to be the defining feature of the next couple of decades.

---

[79]The term "generations" on Google Trends Search increases significantly beginning in 2011 and onward. Search on July 24, 2019, https://trends.google.com/trends/explore?date=all&geo=US&q=generations

Tech Millionaires and Billionaires and Generational Change

The image of a young tech millionaire or billionaire from a cool new startup had become cliché by the mid-'00s. Steve Jobs, Bill Gates, Paul Allen, Larry Ellison, Michael Dell were some of the best known of the young and wealthy tech billionaires in the '90s. A steady stream of headlines and other stories about these millionaires and billionaires altered public perceptions of tech workers. The early '90s image of a socially awkward Computer Science nerd was fading fast.

This new tech wealth quickly made the industry appear more glamorous and cool than was imagined possible during the '70s or '80s. Lots of kids in high school or college, who were not inclined to technology growing up, sought out ways to get a tech job. This worked well for some and less well for others. During college, I remember students switching their major to Computer Science or Information Technology, only to switch to something less technical after learning to code overwhelmed them. Kids that chose the more realistic paths tended to be more successful.

In 2017 half of the world's 174 tech billionaires lived in Silicon Valley.[80] Young millionaires were popping up all over, but mostly in Silicon Valley and areas of the country connected to the tech industry. Most young millionaires did not seek out media self-promotion media attention, but they do tend to stay close to each other and this holds up over time.

The reactions to this nouveau riche were similar to reactions to newly acquired wealth historically. Some would see the youth and success of these tech millionaires and felt motivation while others felt jealousy.

Age was a key factor in whether people saw a tech millionaire as a source of inspiration or resentment. The younger people often saw it

---

[80]This is according to research by Wealth-X as reported in Recode on May 19, 2018. https://www.recode.net/2018/5/19/17370288/silicon-valley-how-many-billionaires-start-up-tech-bay-area

as inspiration because the tech world was open to them and they could learn to succeed in it. The older you were the less that was the case.

Many in the Boomer generation were typical of this generation gap. They did feel much of the excitement, but also a tinge of jealousy and resentment for not being positioned to fully take part in this wave of wealth creation.

My dad had been working for 20 years at the Seattle branch of the Federal Securities and Exchange Commission (SEC). After retiring from the SEC he then worked independently as a successful certified public accountant (CPA). But when the dotcom boom really got going in the late '90s, he was already over 50. The age and culture gap between his generation and those starting companies posed a difficult obstacle.

Understandably, many workers felt awestruck that a young generation had done the modern equivalent of striking gold or oil in a previous era. But there was also frustration because in this new economy there was an implied tech literacy and culture barrier that was harder to learn the older you were.

Many tech millionaires made their money while still in their 20s or 30s. Their youth made it easier to avoid some of the social exclusivity associated with money if they chose to. The youthful nouveau riche in Silicon Valley was probably the most chill, laid back, friendly, open, and down to earth set of newly wealthy individuals that ever existed.

The image from the early '90s of computer science geeks, spending all night alone in a dark room staring at a brightly glowing computer screen gulping Mountain Dew had by the early '00s transitioned to that of a sharp, youthful, problem-solver exuding confidence and possessing powerful skills that could produce enormous wealth.

Sounds of a Generation

The music world that opened up to me in late 1995 was comprised of cool radio DJs who were often obnoxious, cigarette smoke-filled rooms packed with colliding bodies in moshpits, t-shirts with band names everywhere, CD and record stores that hadn't changed much for decades, and endless arguments over the best band. Rock music was definitely in its final days of being a dominant cultural force.

Among my friends at the time, we didn't realize or care what phase of growth rock music was in. We spent afternoons analyzing rock albums and arguing which bands were more original and which were imitating posers.

In the fall of 1995, I was sick and at home from school one day and I ended up watching a lot of music videos on MTV. A new song "Just a Girl" by No Doubt was on MTV's heavy rotation and I must have watched it 4–5 times that day. Smashing Pumpkins' video, "Bullet With Butterfly Wings," was also just released and was played repeatedly throughout the day. Other videos, like Presidents of the USA's "Peaches" and Everclear's "Santa Monica," got plenty of airplay on MTV and radio stations across the country. This music is like a soundtrack of late '95 and early '96 to me.

When songs went on heavy rotation on MTV, the effect was powerful, like when something goes viral on the Internet today. One day to the next it just enters public conscious and quickly everyone seemingly knows about it.[81] The song would quickly show up on the radio, in conversations, in class, work, everywhere.

I liked all this music and found it easy to identify with although I didn't buy any of their albums. I did like their music, it was on radio stations I listened to and it was music that my friends would also listen to and talk about. These were all guitar rock bands with some mix of electric guitar, bass guitar, drums, and vocals.

As a kid trying to figure out whether you actually liked a certain genre of music, it seemed there were some tremendous societal pressures of previous decades telling you that this was the music you should be listening to. Maybe it was just the right kind of music for me or good corporate marketing, but even though I liked the music, it seemed like a foregone conclusion that this is the music I, and people similar to me, should like and buy.

You felt a sense of obligation to the artists and like in some way you were voting for artists to become popular. You also felt like you were consciously deciding to join a club. Many of these same social

---

[81] This is primarily true among the targeted groups of the content.

pressures are at play on the Internet. It is society's social pressures and cultural exposure all intermixed with acute commercial interest.

Internet advertising helps content find the right people; create a group and even a sense of belonging. However, the Internet enables precise targeting of who sees which information more exactly than imagined possible in earlier mediums of advertising and promotion. The ability to leverage advertising to make people feel strong attachments to music, products, and ideas has been amplified immensely with the Internet.[82]

During the '90s, record labels were relying on well-established but inefficient marketing techniques by today's standards. Nobody got big and famous without the assent of a recording label. Production and distribution of music had been so commercialized that any success was not accidental. And any big sensation, like Nirvana, was quickly copied, watered down, and commoditized. The Internet threatened this business model, which by the '90s had been sustained for decades.

Someone reading this who was a teenager in the '90s can remember big stacks of CD's in their bedroom or their friends' bedroom. Cassette tapes were still around but vanishing quickly, they were mostly just used as mixtapes to listen to in the car. Usually, you got a CD of music because you at least liked a song or two. Everyone experienced the pain of buying a CD based on a song you heard on the radio, or saw on MTV, to end up finding out most of the album was just filler.

I remember in mid-1995 going to my friend Jacob's house. He was probably the biggest music enthusiast of anyone I knew at the time. He was in the same grade but went to a different middle school. He had made this large poster, about 3 feet wide and 2.5 feet tall with band names, logos, and pictures. It was mostly newer rock and alternative rock. It had: Pearl Jam, Oasis, Alice in Chains, Nirvana, Metallica, U2, Smashing Pumpkins, Bush, Green Day, Alanis Morisette, Hootie

---

[82] Chamath Palihapitiya, early Facebook employee, gave a long warning on the negative effects of online advertising at the Stanford Graduate School of Business in November of 2017, https://www.youtube.com/watch?v=PMotykw0SIk&feature=youtu.be

and the Blowfish,[83] and some classic rock acts like Led Zeppelin and Aerosmith.

At the time I'd heard of most of the names on Jacob's poster, even though I couldn't think of specific songs. I mostly just went off the impressions I had of the style of each band. I was just beginning to listen to music on the radio and this led to talking about music, and this, of course, this led to arguing about music.

In the summer of 1995, the Internet was still a ways off from being used regularly for instant fact checking. So we would argue about where bands with our opinions being informed by what older siblings said, other kids at school said, what we remembered from a magazine, or what some radio DJ or MTV host said. This is what it was like before facts were easy to find online. You argued more intensely because you knew the true facts couldn't be known.

Smartphone Fact-Checking

When smartphone fact-checking finally came to be a thing, it was in the late '00s. For kids born in the '80s, one can only wonder how it may have changed so many arguments during High School or college had it been available. People began to regularly do smartphone fact checks in the middle of both heated arguments and polite discussions. This did usually deescalate the arguments or end discussions. By the time smartphones had become popular people had come to trust the information on the Internet.

One behavioral change from fact-checking in arguments is that we ended up caring less about the deeper truth, and more about the facts that were presented online, leading us to care less about each other. This is probably why so much social media material began to be

---

[83]Jacob made this poster in 1995, when Hootie and the Blowfish were still considered cool. In 1996, when I saw this and commented, "Hootie, really?" he responded, "Shut up, man! You used to like them, too." Jacob was also really into Alannis Morrissette, mostly because he, like many others, had a crush on her. A couple years later she changed her image drastically, but at the time, she, along with Gwen Stefani from No Doubt, were both the quintessential teenage heartthrobs.

focused on making us feel emotions. Whether it was anger, jealousy, deep curiosity, these were all emotions more likely to get us to engage. Over time, this encouraged more sensational stories to be featured more prominently.

But, ultimately, it was human connection that people craved and often felt detached from, even while a lot of information online became tailor-made to drive up emotions. But, since we discussed and argued less in person, we lost some of the ability to nuance and articulate our ideas; it was all about what the Internet said.

Internet Rumors: The Source and the Solution

It should be noted that it still took years (between 1995 through the popularity of smartphones beginning in 2007) for information on the Internet to become widely accepted as reliable. Throughout the '90s, a common running joke went like this: Someone would make a ridiculous claim like, "Polar bears are living in the wild in Florida"; and then someone would respond with, "Really? Now where did you hear about that?" And the response would come, "I found it on the Internet somewhere."

In the late '90s, it was obvious the Internet could provide some of the best information. Rumors and stories would be exaggerated easily. A rumor could be placed on a website and spread quickly to many more eyeballs than would be possible in traditional media or person-to-person methods. There were numerous falsely reported celebrity deaths, whether by mistake or as a hoax for clickbait, during this period.[84] Sorting through the good and bad information was time-consuming, and there was certainly a generational difference in who understood how to use and manipulate the Internet for their own purposes.

However, by 2005, the tide had been turning for trusting the Internet. Wikipedia was quickly gaining broader acceptance as being nearly

---

[84]Wikipedia entry on premature reported deaths. https://en.wikipedia.org/wiki/List_of _premature_obituaries

as reliable as an encyclopedia.[85] Before Google and Wikipedia became mainstream and established strong algorithms to vet websites and remove much of the bad or unreliable information, most people thought the Internet was about as likely to give you good or bad information.

And a few years later, by the time smartphones became popularized, the internet was well passed the inflection point of being more widely trusted than distrusted.

---

[85] Published in 2005, Thomas Friedman's book, *The World is Flat*, has a section comparing entries found in Wikipedia and an encyclopedia. The accuracy on Wikipedia was not only nearly as good but also improving at a faster rate than possible for published books.

CHAPTER TEN

INTERNET MEDIA GENERATION

Nearly everyone applauded how the Internet made information instantly accessible to everyone, and basically for free. As the access, quality, and speed of information improved people came to rely less and less on a few preferred media outlets for facts and information. Faced with greater competition, media outlets, especially TV, found that facts and information were becoming devalued. To retain their audience media outlets changed their presentation of facts and information to be more immediate, emotionally sensational, and continuous.

These emotional contortions blur facts and information but in the post-Internet information-rich environment in which we began to live, this is what viewers responded to. The weakened our ability to discern, understand, and respond appropriately to information.

By the mid-'00s people began to focus more heavily on the particular news sources that best reinforced their perspective. People entered these information siloes of sorts. This was done consciously and also unconsciously. This newly competitive Internet media landscape gave birth to many opportunities for people in the rising generation that better understood how to get attention on the Internet while also simultaneously ending, abruptly, the careers of media workers who were less inclined.

Newspaperless Generation

In the summer of 1998, I was 16 and excited to finally be able to work. At the end of the school year, I saw an ad on a school billboard for a job that paid $9 an hour at a Nintendo assembly warehouse. I called the temporary employment agency and went in to interview a couple days later. They were thrown off by my young age, as most workers at the Nintendo warehouse were in their '30s. To get to the Nintendo factory I drove 45 minutes out to North Bend, 30 miles east of Seattle, where the Nintendo assembly warehouse was located. I worked 13-hour shifts stuffing video games into cardboard packages.[86]

The work was repetitive and physically demanding. You felt your legs, hands, and especially the joints on your fingers get stiff throughout the day. Out of the roughly 50 people working on the assembly line, I was the youngest as far as I could tell, although there were a few others just out of high school or in their early 20s.

On the assembly line coworkers are usually open to talking about almost anything. When you rely on people around you for some kind of conversation to help you make it through a 13-hour shift, there's a mutual interest in talking and being open. There was generally less pretense and worry over internal politics than what I have found in more formal corporate and office environments.

Waking up at 5 am, commuting 45 minutes, and returning at about 8 pm just to go to sleep and do it all over again would be a shock to the system for most teenagers. But I loved that I was making money and able to work. Even though I thought the job was fine, I also wondered about what other jobs were out there since I had found the job so quickly.

I looked around the classified ads section in *The Seattle Times*, the largest newspaper in Seattle. My family had subscribed to *The Seattle Times* on and off for years. My older brother had a paper route for about 30 homes when I was about 10. He made about $250 a month and I sometimes helped him with it.

Before the Internet, newspapers classified advertising section was a great place to find a job. As a kid, I looked at the classified ads in newspapers all the time to find a dog or other pet to adopt. Beginning

---

[86] When I saw the name of the Nintendo game we were packaging and shipping I had never even heard of it. Up to that point, I assumed that I would recognize most Nintendo games but soon realized the gaming world had grown significantly since the early '90s.

in the early '00s, Craigslist and other online classified sites began stealing away much of newspapers classified advertising.

One day, in the *Seattle Times* newspaper I found a large quarter-page ad that claimed you could make $15 an hour doing door-to-door sales. The job was working for *The Seattle Times* sales team, which is probably why they always had a large ad covering a quarter of the newspaper page.

I called the number listed right away, trying to make myself sound good over the phone (radio classes in High School helped with that). On the phone, the team manager for the Seattle eastside area claimed that most salesmen made around $15–$20 an hour and that I could come in to meet the new team manager the following week. I went in the next week to a nondescript office park right next to the main Microsoft[87] campus on the border of Redmond and Bellevue.

I met with a fairly new sales team manager named Stan McAllister, who soon became my first boss. During our interview, I remember that he said, "I've always had the top sales team" in a way that really showed he intended to keep it that way. I was the first person he interviewed and since he was building out his new team he gave me a job offer a few days later, despite having no prior sales experience.

On my first day of work, I got a sale at one of the first houses I knocked. It was in a residential area of Kirkland, a suburb of Seattle. That sale earned me about $21, more than the $9 in an hour on the assembly line at Nintendo. It was awkward bothering people in their home, but breathing that fresh Seattle air, seeing new areas of the city, not being in a warehouse, and making more money was all very appealing. Within a couple weeks I left the job at Nintendo.

On that first night selling in 1998, it was also clear that news was shifting online. I remember one interaction I had, after giving my sales pitch: "Hello, I'm from *The Seattle Times* and I would like to offer you the Sunday newspaper for $1.85 with the rest of the week absolutely free

---

[87]Within a few months of this time, Microsoft expanded its main campus forcing all tenants in this office park to move to other locations.

of charge" the guy at the door just responded calmly, "No thanks. We have the news on the Internet, so we don't really need the paper."

The same day I discovered a better way to make money was also the same day that I learned it wouldn't last many years longer.[88] The fate of newspapers was obvious, even if the timing wasn't.

During the next two years, I earned a decent income with this part-time evening job walking around neighborhoods around the Seattle metropolitan area. As time progressed I heard versions of that same response I got on my first day more often. "We don't need it, we get the news online," or "Everything's online now, don't need to kill a tree and have those papers piling up," and similar explanations.

The question of the future of newspapers kept coming up: "What will the Internet do to newspapers?" and "What will online news look like in the future?" The question was clearly directed at the timing—"when," not "if," the Internet will replace newspapers.

Looking back, it is more surprising to me that newspapers held on as long as they did. The costs of turning trees into paper, printing colored ink onto miles of paper, and then slicing that up, stacking them, sending them out on trucks, and then into bundles to be hand-delivered to millions of houses every day. This is horribly inefficient, since the sheets on most papers made, were never even used!

When people did read newspapers, it was usually just the front page and maybe a couple articles from the only section they were actually interested in (Sports, Entertainment, Crossword, Classifieds), meanwhile, the rest of the paper went to waste.

Between 1998–2000 I encountered more and more people that said they would never get newspapers delivered. In nerdy and tech-heavy Seattle this change likely hit a bit earlier than other cities around the country and world. But this trend played out worldwide as newspapers lost subscribers and influence with each year in the '00s.

---

[88] These door-to-door sales jobs with *The Seattle Times* actually lasted until the fall of 2004, when they were part of a 10% reduction in staff at *The Seattle Times*, according to my former boss.

There was definitely a generational difference. In 2007 the director of my department at US Airways, who was around 45, complained in multiple meetings, "You young people don't subscribe to newspapers. How do you know anything?"

As someone who actually liked newspapers, it did appear that something was being lost and felt some sympathy for journalists writing about their own declining industry. The articles you would see in those first years complaining about the pending demise and increased economic pressures on newspapers raised some interesting points about the value of newspapers to society. But over the years, these kinds of articles by reporters and editorialists became more desperate, spiteful, and angry.

After about 2005 the articles from desperate journalists decrying the loss of newspapers, or arguing for some resurgence seemed borderline delusional. Sure, there may have been some loss from people not the reading news as deeply, but it was not practical to expend vast resources to save printed newspapers. Many of these articles that I read sounded more like years of writing expertise put into a diatribe exuding pain over diminished career prospects rather than a journalistic take on a new reality by examining realistic solutions.

While declining job prospects was an obvious annoyance to the frontline journalists, what was not obvious to most people but I believe a key driving factor of what really got under the skin of newspaper owners and editorialists was the loss of power and influence.[89] A primary source of scorn was the loss of power to many new people who were perceived as younger and more tech-savvy but supposedly less cultured, intellectual, and deserving. This psychological pain of loss and the fears associated with what lies next compelled owners and editorialists to hang on as long as possible.

---

[89] Many of the owners, executives, and editorialists did fine economically in the new digital economy. But it was the loss of influence (people caring about your opinion) is what was more difficult to replace for many of these previously important people. Frontline journalists, operations and distribution staff at many small and midsized newspapers probably bore most the brunt of newspaper consolidation and downsizing in the '00s.

In 2009 I was speaking with an attorney a few years older than me who summed up the online news situation concisely "our generation is not going to be subscribing to newspapers."

In late 2010 I remember reading a short piece in *The Economist* magazine[90] on the fate of the newspaper industry. It was brief, pragmatic, and written in a way that was fully aware that print newspapers would not exist in the same capacity going forward, with just details to be settled.

It took well over a decade for most of journalism to accept the new reality of the Internet and digital era, but after 2010, the inevitable reality was generally acknowledged and understood.

The Power of Blogs

By 2005, a large portion of people relied on the Internet for much of their news.[91] By then, most news outlets had a well-functioning website where you could read most of their articles. Around this same time, news sites began competing with something called weblogs, better known as "blogs."

Most people who wrote blog posts in these years, myself included, were just spouting off ideas on whatever interested them at the moment. It was a great for those with ideas or thoughts that you just had to get out into the world, or at least to an audience that was a small group of friends. Quality was mixed, but that didn't matter. It was so easy and fun to create blog posts that people spent hours writing and reading blogs, at night after work and more often during work.

Though a lot of the writing, pictures and other content were nonsense, blogs quickly became a conduit for some of the most valuable online interactions.

The big value of blogs was that they could open up access to experts. This enabled the sharing of expertise and specialized knowledge

---

[90] It has been debated whether *The Economist* is a newspaper or magazine. The entity has asserted that it is a newspaper. However, during a job interview that I had with the former CEO Andrew Rashbass in 2009, Rashbass referred to the publication as a magazine.
[91] According to my former sales manager, the door-to-door sales unit at *The Seattle Times* was eliminated in the fall of 2004.

on a variety of topics that had been particularly complex or out of reach for most people. One reason for this is that many experts on a topic are not exceptional writers. But the knowledge they can share is far more valuable than what a journalist with years of experience could attempt to portray in a short article.

Before blogs, these experts, in most instances, had to filter their ideas through specific journalists with limited specialization at media outlets that have narrow audience interests and commercial constraints. Inevitably, these journalists and media outlets would water down the words, ideas, and concepts in attempts to better couch them into a catchy story in addition to other constraints inherent to for-profit media outlets. In the better case scenarios in this process, the readers were entertained, but the larger interests of the public, such as having access to the best information in its pure form, was rarely served.

Ideally, a journalist makes the ideas and information of an expert more interesting, useful, and relevant than an expert could. But it's often the case that since journalists are trained to tell stories; they filter out the genius of an expert when formatting the information to fit a story. In other words, some things are just complex and dressing it up with pretty language can be a major disservice to telling the truth.

Moreover, journalists are rarely experts on the topics they write about. This is especially true of more technical topics. They often develop some expertise in explaining their topics making them appealingly to their target audience. But as many areas of work have become far more technical and detailed it less likely there will be writers with the innate ability, or time and resources, to develop a dual specialty on most topics they write about. This is especially the case in more tech-focused and science-driven fields.

So blogs became a fantastic workaround to get the best explanations that were direct from the source. They were usually far from the best written, but the information was in its purest, and often most valuable form.

Some blogs made by experts in topics like finance, travel, entertainment, law, or music became very popular because readers liked having that media filter removed. People wanted access to expertise, skipping the now unnecessary intermediary, that's the core of what made the Internet so great. Traditional news media often had too many editorial limitations to provide the cutting edge information, non-consensus opinions, or specialized knowledge until it had been broadly accepted. On this front, blogs could get far ahead of most media. Some bloggers did try to compete with reporting day to day news issues, with some success. A term used frequently at this time was "citizens journalism" or "Micro Reporting" to describe unpaid bloggers writing about their communities. Around this time, Newspapers across the US were drastically reducing or eliminating local news coverage. To respond to the demand for local news, people, who were not experienced writers, started using blogs to share what was happening in their part of town. Why would people spend hours doing this for free? Because what is more satisfying than talking about the place you care about most, the place where you live?

I started a blog in early 2007 while I was an intern at the United Nations headquarters in New York City. The title was way too long, "aviewoftheworld.blogspot.com." I wrote about my experiences at the United Nations, New York, and whatever else came to mind during that winter and spring. About a dozen friends regularly viewed or commented on my posts and an occasional random person would come across it and say something, usually positive.

While writing this blog, I did pick up on some patterns about Internet behavior that have held up over time. I wrote a post about Croatia, which prior to the *Game of Thrones* HBO series was not a place that people in the US cared about. The post was basically ignored. After *Game of Thrones* came out, Croatia was a topic that people responded to.

When I posted anything involving New York City, this triggered a bunch of comments and reactions. Whether positive or negative most people have some reaction to New York City. People respond to what triggers emotional responses and this tends to be places, things, and ideas, they are familiar with or they see other people responding to.

Like most bloggers, after about a year my posts became less frequent and as I ran short on ideas I stopped posting. For a while, it was a great way to practice articulating ideas and a fantastic conversation starter. The best blogs tended to endure the longest. For me, the biggest lesson of blogs was the value of unfiltered specialized information.

CHAPTER ELEVEN

THE GAMING REVOLUTION

In 1985, the Nintendo Entertainment System was launched in the US test markets of New York and Los Angeles. Within a year Nintendo was distributed throughout much of North America. By 1990, talk about Nintendo probably comprised about half of the conversations amongst male students at my Elementary School. We talked about special passwords for *Zelda* or how to get past "Bald Bull" in *Mike Tyson's: Punch-Out*. We argued all the time about the best of the *Mario* games and what made playing *Metroid* or *Bubble Bobble* so fun.[92]

During the late '80s and '90s, kids devoted an enormous amount of time playing Nintendo and Sega. If you added it all up, kids with Nintendo and Sega gaming sets in their home spent hundreds if not thousands of hours playing or watching people play. When parents got worried about the potentially harmful effects of their kids sitting and playing games for too long, we just repeated a line that playing Nintendo improved "hand-eye coordination." At the time, we barely understood what this phrase meant, so we couldn't realize the fact that any physical activity can improve hand-eye coordination.

Most of the time playing Nintendo the only physical activity was using your eyeballs to track movements on the screen and pressing buttons on the controllers. I remember one time my grandfather was

---

[92] In 2016, capitalizing on Nintendo nostalgia, a miniature-sized Nintendo box with over 300 Nintendo games was released by a Chinese company. The price was $25. After playing some of the top games a few times, the excitement and nostalgia wore thin.

visiting our house. He sat down and watched me play *Rush-n-Attack* for what to me didn't seem too long. Eventually, he exclaimed with some exasperation "You have played that game for five solid hours."

There was a strong social component to playing Nintendo as kids. At school, we would ask old friends and kids we met on the playground, "Hey, do you want to come over after school and play Nintendo?"

If someone got a new game, especially a cool game that was getting hyped up, they would soon find lots of new friends. Often kids would find out you had a new game through another friend and then invite themselves over to play, "you just got the new *Mega Man*?! Can we play it at your house after?!"

Knowing how to beat certain games or hard levels of games made you very popular. My neighbor and friend Robert had this cousin who new all the special moves and how to get past the level bosses for *Teenage Mutant Ninja Turtles* and other secrets. We called him over for help whenever we could.

Somehow, everyone was acutely aware of the social hierarchy, who was cool enough to go to whose house, and who knew the games best. Playing video games did break down some of these social barriers, if only temporarily. Controlling animated characters on screens was somehow magical to our 7 to 12-year-old brains. Playing the newest and best games was more important than the social hierarchy.

It seemed like every kid from my school knew the secret code for 30 lives in *Contra*. I still know it today: "Up-up, down-down, left-right, left-right, B-A, B-A, select-start" for the two-player version. I have no idea how everyone knew it, it must have been published in some gaming magazines and then passed along by word of mouth. With that code, beating the game was fun and a breeze. Without it, the game was basically impossible.

Many of the games had Cold War themes. The game *Rush-n-Attack*, for example, was created in 1985 and was obviously based on fighting in Soviet Russia. The hats and uniforms on every enemy soldier in the game look distinctly Russian, even to an eight-year-old. The music style and patriotic imagery was such a product of its Cold War environment that it's hard to imagine a game like that being made again.

Nintendo put out more complex games and an array of fantasy-themed games, *Zelda*, *Dragon Warrior*, *Final Fantasy* came out that could be played solo for hours. These games built on a genre that had been growing since the success of fantasy novels like *Lord of the Rings* in the late 1950s. The popularity of fantasy role-playing style games like *Dungeons and Dragons* in the '70s and '80s had an enormous impact on the gaming community. This laid some of the foundation and interest and technical capacity in designing fantasy-themed games on Nintendo and other gaming platforms.

The global video gaming explosion of the '80s drove hundreds of millions of kids, and adults in total to eventually spend billions of hours playing games on TV screens. If you also take into consideration how much time people also spent thinking or talking about those games, the global time invested is probably significantly higher. For those born in the '80s, video gaming replaced cartoons and TV as the most time consuming and mentally absorbing activity.

Arcades were still around in the early '90s, but they were vanishing as younger kids had game systems at home. Arcades seemed to cater to an older crowd. The interior designs looked anachronistic. Most were built in the '70s or early '80s with little invested in updating them. They looked like they belonged in a different era.

Successful arcade games usually had a Nintendo or Sega version of the game. Arcades were still sort of cool to stop by once in a while especially if it meant going for a bike ride and getting away. But there were few arcades near where I lived, so I didn't go often.

There were fewer arcade games produced in the '90s, but the games that were made were a lot flashier and with better graphics and sound systems. Perhaps this was because arcades had to compete with Nintendo and Sega for the rising generation of gamers. Attracting and holding kid's attention in an arcade was harder and so you, therefore, needed something exceptional. At the arcades that did exist in 1990, the gaming experience was far superior to what *Pac-Man* got you for 25¢ in 1980, and cost more too. And the games cost more, most games were 50¢ or a dollar in the '90s.

Between 1990 and 2000, arcade games in convenience stores like 7-Eleven and mom and pops shops almost vanished. Standalone arcades were fewer in number. If there was an arcade it was usually just a section of a big gaming complex or in the lobby of a larger store.

In 1997, specialty arcades such as GameWorks were popping up and promoted a modern and socially engaging gaming experience. GameWorks in Seattle was located downtown had a futuristic look that more like a place you could hang out with your friends all night compared with how the dated and stodgy arcades looked. Importantly, at GameWorks many of the games were multiplayer and the whole store layout was group-oriented. This emphasized the social aspect of gaming, which had been somewhat lost with Nintendo as many gamers spent more time at home gaming alone.

The post Internet gaming experience had to be different to hold people's attention. As the video game entertainment gave way to Internet gaming and entertainment it was clear that any gaming store with a physical location should focus on the social setup of gaming to pull people away from their home gaming devices. Modern arcades, like GameWorks, represented a broader shift towards using gaming to bring people together.

Gaming Moves to Computers and Online

Meanwhile, the original Nintendo Entertainment System was replaced by the Super Nintendo in 1993, which was later replaced by the Nintendo 64 in 1996.[93] During the '90s Nintendo had to stay fresh by improving the speed, graphics as technology made this possible, and also compete to continue to produce cool games.

When I played Nintendo as a kid, we would gather at somebody's house and take turns playing *Mario*, *Zelda*, *Contra* or whichever game.

---

[93] Nintendo did produce many other notable devices including the portable GameBoy and some less popular consoles.

Since there were usually three, four or more of us kids from the neighborhood and most games were just a single-player, we sat and watched and helped like it was a collective effort. So a lot of time was spent waiting to play.

When the Nintendo 64 came out, in 1996, gaming on computers had improved a lot from ten years earlier when the original Nintendo came out, and attention and investment were shifting in that direction. The early computer games were slow, had poor graphics and playability because there was no handheld controller.

Also, a big limitation was that games couldn't work on your computer because of compatibility issues. Also, most computer screens were much smaller than TVs. It just was not practical for many games, especially multiplayer games that could be more of a social experience. Consequently, computer gaming early on was much less social and more isolating.

The Nintendo 64 had a clear advantage in competing with Computer Games for the multiplayer gaming experience. But despite some notably awesome exceptions, like *MarioKart*, *GoldenEye*, and *BomberMan 64*, there were few Nintendo 64 games of lasting significance from this time period. Unfortunately for Nintendo, this window of opportunity would close within a few years as the Internet-enabled online gaming started to really take off.

As the number of computer games increased during the 90s the social component of gaming decreased. We still talked about games quite a bit, but we got together to play them less often. First-person shooter computer games became hugely popular, especially with teenagers and college-age guys. Initially, these games were played solo, against computer opponents.

The first widely successful first-person shooter game at the time was *Wolfenstein 3D* in 1992. Wolfenstein was followed by a succession of hugely popular first-person shooter games: *Doom* in 1993, then *Quake* in 1996, *Counter-Strike* in 2000, *Halo* in 2001, and *Call of Duty* in 2003.

The game *Quake*, which came out in 1996, allowed a multi-player online mode. This multiplayer online mode would become very important in the following years as Internet speeds improved. At the time, though, playing *Quake* online was usually too slow and with too few other people who could play it with you online.

When *Counter-Strike* came out, in 2000, the timing was better. Internet and computer processing speeds were faster, graphics were better, and it became very popular. By 2000, online speeds could better keep up with the speed of play and game quality. *Halo*, which came out in late 2001, followed by *Call of Duty* in 2003 also set high standards for multi-person shooter games.

As these games improved and more people had fast broadband Internet, just playing solo against the computer became predictable and boring. You would get the new game, play it, maybe spend some time and beat it once, and then only play the game in multiplayer.

Some people reading this will remember LAN parties when you would all hook up to play against others in the same room. It was so much more fun to play against a bunch of your buddies in the same room or against other people online than just playing against the computer. You could form teams, trash talk, making it more fun than playing against the computer.

Kids born in the late '80s and early '90s did most their gaming on computers. My brother Blake, born in 1988, played some Nintendo, but mostly it was online multiplayer games where gaming really came to life. I remember the summer of 2007, on most days he played for several hours, before lunch, the game *Rome: Total War*, *World of Warcraft*, and other multiplayer games.

After playing a game in an online multiplayer for a while most gamers didn't want to go back to just playing against the computer. They would say things like "playing against the computer is boring, I can predict exactly what the computer is going to do every time." Playing against humans is still far more exciting because the psychological challenge and element of surprise make it more fun.

Perhaps Artificial Intelligence (AI) and Machine Learning will advance enough to reverse this trend. Perhaps in the coming years, AI programmed games and multiplayer opponents will improve to exceed the experience of playing against another human. Perhaps playing against AI opponents on multiplayer be more exciting and fun than playing against other humans because the AI will be especially matched against each human player's particular playing abilities.

Other big computer-based strategy games like WarCraft, 1994, and StarCraft, 1998, both made by Blizzard Entertainment, were very popular. StarCraft has stood the test of time and maintained global popularity. A key innovation to keeping this game alive was the "battlenet" which is an online portal where you play against other people online. You could set up games against friends or random people. And you could play against anyone, anywhere in the world, any time of day. Blizzard also created the immensely popular role-playing style game World of Warcraft.

Gaming became much more competitive as you began to compare yourself to the best players from the world, not just the kids in your neighborhood like back in the 80s. It took almost no time for it to feel absolutely normal to play against teams on the other side of the US or in South Korea. The person you played against or teamed up with was faceless and voiceless, and usually they had some cryptic code name. Often the only communication came through an acronym at the end "gg" (good game). We felt equal, regardless of language or country of origin, because we were all just be judged strictly off gaming ability.

Reputations and patterns soon emerged. Korean kids quickly earned a reputation as being revered StarCraft players. They were tough to play against, so you were happy to have them on your team. Years later, in 2007, I learned from some Korean intern friends that in South Korea there was a whole industry of "professional" gamers who actually made a living playing in StarCraft competitions in South Korea.

In the US gaming may never be as widely respected as gaming in South Korea.[94] This is one difference that seemed very interesting.

---

[94] I visited South Korea in mid-2008 at the age of 26. Technology appeared to permeate society more than the United States or any other country. In parks, on the subway, and other public areas it looked like everyone, old and young, saw technology as something that was interlinked with their life. I remember riding on a deep underground subway and seeing a lady in her 70s watching a live TV program on a portable TV, something you would not see in the US at the time.

Lots of Korean girls I met appeared comfortable with guys who played *StarCraft* regularly either for fun or a job. Girls in the US, at least when I was in high school, thought it was pretty strange if guys were playing games like *StarCraft*. Even at 15, I remember it was obvious that a decent number of kids played these games but it was definitely not something you talked about around girls or people who didn't play. South Korea is a great example of a country where the Internet culture and Online Gaming culture has permeated through society much faster and more fully than in the United States.

Online Gaming and Language

In the book *Tractatus Logico-Philosophicus*, Ludwig Wittgenstein argues that an inherent problem of language is the rudimentary limitations of words to create a mutual understanding. In other words, the struggle of language is conveying the thoughts and feelings in a way that those precise thoughts and feelings will be transmitted from one person to another. With this insight, online communication tactics and tools like: GIFs, emojis, abbreviations, and sending short videos are all ways to leverage new technological capacity to express thoughts and feelings through the Internet medium.

GIFs can usually make you feel an emotion quicker and stronger than trying to write out a clumsy sentence or paragraph. GIFs have become a powerful means to express a shared reference. Since they are visual they are particularly useful for a generation of adults that have generally spent a vastly greater amount of time watching TV, movies, and Internet videos than reading Greek classics, history, poetry, or other oft-quoted literary sources in previous generations. A GIF more quickly conjures up the intended feelings by associating it with a well known, or easily understood, TV or movie scene.

GIFs and emojis also help to solve at least two modern language limitations.

1. *Shorter attention spans.* This limits the ability to understand complex ideas, which by necessity must be expressed through large blocks of text, which people hate reading or even look at.

2. *Reduced emotionality.* As mentioned earlier in this book, the increase in time spent staring at screens has correlated with a reduction in people's ability to express emotions with body language. Using a GIF to show actors making exaggerated expressions is a kind of shortcut to expressing and transmitting those emotions yourself.

A whole set of online language patterns emerged as people spent more time online especially for specific purposes or online communities like gaming. As is common with any language adaptation, using acronyms and abbreviations in online fora is part of showing which online communities you want to belong to, and which partly determines if you'll be accepted. "Newbie" "lol" "spam" "gg" and writing in "CAPS LOCK" being equivalent to shouting were some of the first and most enduring online speech patterns.

In any online communication, Facebook event, group chat, job applications and interviews, Twitter comments, and anything else, the ability to express yourself online involves using language for social positioning. The fact that we have only in recent years begun to have the Internet tools that permit communicating in ways approximating real-life communications (ex: FaceTime) means we have a way to go in developing these language patterns. There is so much to be optimistic about online communications improve and become more seamless with real life opening opportunities to use language in ways that more similar to real life.

Gaming and Play

Play is fundamental to the human experience. How we learn to play as a kid shapes a lifetime of our mental and social habits, behavior, and growth.

A game can be defined as a set of rules used to achieve defined outcomes. Games can be played alone, with other people, or with artificial intelligence. Playing games can produce powerful chemical rewards and the games that produce the best rewards the most consistently are the ones we return to the most. The most engaging and rewarding over time have been social games, played with multiple people.[95]

The gaming process of following rules to achieve defined outcomes is built into our use of language. We learn a set of rules, and in speaking, writing, and other non-verbal communication we try to achieve defined outcomes. We adapt our communication based on the responses of the person, or people, playing. We are constantly following rules, whether consciously or unconsciously, and constantly being evaluated and judged on how well we follow these rules.[96]

People I know who were born in the '80s often remark how they are grateful that they grew up in a time without the Internet because it allowed them to have a 'normal' childhood. Most kids who grew up before the Internet experienced gaming and play with other kids, often in-person and face to face.

Kids born in the '80s did play a lot of Nintendo, but it was often in a social context. Kids born after the early '90s are much more likely to have spent their time playing games at home alone on a computer.

There was a period of disorientation and isolation. However, I argue that the solution to this lack of socialization was already being developed. As the Internet evolved the chance for kids to interact in meaningful and positive ways with other kids online improved. The process took a couple of decades; this disorientating period where lots of people went online without proper tools to stay connected to other humans in positive ways was roughly from 1995 through 2015.

I believe that after 2015 the Internet socialtools were in place for much better interactions (better voice, video, real-time communication, higher numbers of people). Society will begin to see better and more positive results from Internet interactions, though these positive effects may take some years to be observed, valued, and properly appreciated.

---

[95] According to WorldAtlas.com, the sports with the most worldwide fans are: Soccer 4B, Cricket 2.5B, Field Hockey 2B, Tennis 1B, Volleyball 900M, Table Tennis 875M, Basketball 825M, Baseball 500M, Rugby 475M, Golf 450M https://www.worldatlas.com/articles/what-are-the-most-popular-sports-in-the-world.html

[96] In all of these examples, the rules are affected by many factors. These include the situational context and social expectations of our group.

Online is now the place where most kids learn the social rules for play.

It was long assumed that kids who spent most of their time socializing online, and not in the real world, would be at a disadvantage, socially and professionally, in the game of life. However, we are likely at the point where a better predictor for success in life is not the kids that best learn how to socialize on the playground, but the kids that are the best learners of how to socialize, connect, and play with others in online formats.

Beginning somewhere between 2008 and 2012, kids', and many adults', interactions online were more frequent and of greater significance than their interactions in person. This is the period when the tools to interact, like social media and smartphones, were made available to most people. Since social habits tend to develop at a young age, changes in Internet tools during this time period had greater long-term effects on the younger generations.

Since the gaming platforms interacting were relatively new, the rules of social conduct and decorum were mostly unregulated. It is not surprising that this is the period when online bullying grew to national and international attention. Online bullying can be particularly damaging, for example, teenage girls bullying other teenage girls through shaming, gossiping, and tarnishing the reputation of other teenage girls.[97] Trolling, public shaming, and other negative online behaviors have also been observed by most people in greater frequency after this period.

Eventually, when playing games online the computers became very predictable. You felt like it knew each click and movement you made, so it reacted correspondingly. When you play against human players, what makes it fun is the difficulty of predicting what will happen and the player patterns.

---

[97]This research is still being studied and so far has only been shown increased bullying among teenage girls correlate with the years of increased social media use. Professor Jonathan Haidt elaborates on this research in the Jan 7, 2019 episode of the Joe Rogan podcast: https://www.youtube.com/watch?v=CI6rX96oYnY

Playing against other players of similar ability who did not have pre-programmed moves had an element of surprise that playing against the computer could not reproduce. I remember playing against a series of tough opponents, some that I lost and others that I won, but feeling like I could play forever.[98]

By 2000, Internet cafes with fast speed LAN networks popped up cities and small towns all over the world. Some of this was filling the demand for playing the latest games left by the vanishing arcades. In late 2007, I was in central London and stopped in at an Internet café that was packed with people nearly all day long.

But as people acquired laptops with Wi-Fi and fast speed Internet, the Internet cafes began disappearing quickly. After 2010, I only recall seeing Internet cafes in airports and developing countries. After 2015, most people in developing countries had mobile phones with data connections and Internet cafes became less common.

Isolating or Uniting?

Arcades, Nintendo, computer gaming, internet gaming, and smartphone gaming. Each development served to further isolate us from meaningful human interaction. And as mentioned previously, this change was socially disorientating, since these early innovations to technology were largely isolating us and not yet uniting us.

Between 1990–2010, gaming consoles and Internet gaming did more to isolate than unite us from each other. This dramatically destabilized the development of social habits. You were not in the same room, like in the 80s and early 90s, looking at each other or talking to each other, you were alone in a room, staring at a screen.

Some games, like *Second Life* and *World of WarCraft*, engrossed people in fantasy worlds far removed from their day-to-day existence. As people spent more of their lives on games and less interacting in real

---

[98] But that feeling would fade. An afternoon of staring at the same digital images on a screen could be mind-numbing. When you stood up after playing for three hours, you realized your body felt different, slower, and lethargic. It made breathing fresh air feel more rewarding.

life, they began to use the tools of games to develop social connections that transcended the gaming world. The Internet matured and the gaming systems matured, encouraging wider range player-to-player interaction. I knew several guys who spent much of their day playing games. This was somewhat common during the initial years of the Great Recession of 2008–2010. One guy told me that most of his social interactions were with friends he made from gaming that he'd never met in person. They discussed serious life problems and shared useful advice to each other at a far deeper level than most people he knew in real life.

As smartphones allowed people to remain connected throughout the day many of the smartphone games featured a social component. *Words with Friends*, two-player chess, were just the very tip of the social gaming iceberg. Now there are loads of games that allow simultaneous co-op playing or whatever degree of play you want.

The most successful games will likely be those that unite us rather than isolate us. The implications of this should be a cause for great optimism.

This could be a major contributor to improve human collaboration in all fields of work, cooperation, and discovery. Nevertheless, the values that people bring to those social interactions are crucial and it's not clear if society is inputting the right values into people to create positive outputs.

I finish this chapter remarking just as with gaming in arcades and playing Nintendo and Sega, people joined together and friendships developed, the same will continue to happen with successful Internet-enabled gaming apps..

CHAPTER TWELVE

INTERNET MATURITY

As the Internet matured, it was driven as much by popular websites, apps, or cool content as venture capital. Infrastructure investments were, and remain, foundational to making the Internet faster and accessible. But from its inception, users have had tremendous sway with which websites and Internet products are ultimately successful. Although venture capitalists and big tech companies (Amazon, Google, Apple, Facebook, etc.) have much more control and power over what people do and see on the Internet, this legacy of listening to the voice and influence of the users remains.

The most successful apps and websites gave people what they wanted. It was, and is, people that build apps and determine which are successful, not venture capital. The disproportionate buildup of wealth in Silicon Valley in recent years has distorted the creative process.

In recent years there has been increasing concern that some of the best potential ideas may be more frequently filtered out by venture capital firms or the big tech companies.[99] The criticism focuses on the shift from a startup culture mindset (focused on developing an idea and improving the world) with investors and a big company mindset (focused on quick returns and growing market position).

---

[99] The stifling of creativity in society due to an excessive focus on fast profits and growing wealth is addressed in depth in a near three-hour podcast discussion between Eric Weinstein and Peter Thiel. July 2019, https://www.youtube.com/watch?v=nM9f0W2KD5s

This could clearly sap the creativity of many potential startup founders for the next generation of new ideas.

The Internet has unquestionably entered a higher degree of maturity during the past decade. One evidence of this is the dominant Internet companies: Amazon, Google, Apple Facebook, etc, and the degree of control on the products we see and the price we pay for them. It is far more likely that these few companies will hold power and influence during the next 20 years than the key players in the Internet world 20 years ago (e.g., Yahoo! and AOL).

Up through the late '90s, and well into the '00s for many people, the Internet was thought of as a scary space full of untrustworthy information and unknown and potentially dangerous people. Human interactions and expressions were often limited to what you read in gimmicky-looking online forums or chatrooms. Much of the Internet looked like it was set up not for humans, but computers, because it was initially. The '90s saw the Internet gradually move out of that space.

Strengths and Weaknesses
We now understand far better what the Internet can do and what it can't.

In the early years of the Internet, there was an excess of optimism that the Internet could do anything and everything, for anyone, anywhere. This vague optimism could be seriously misleading. It has played a part in many of the overhyped investments and failures.

Did people want to buy things online? Yes. Did everyone want to make all their purchases online? No. Did people enjoy interacting online? Yes. Could online interaction substitute all human-to-human interactions? Absolutely not. Can people learn online? Absolutely. Is it better than learning in person or experientially? Depends.

Between 1995–2015 (roughly) finding the right balance to these three questions has been at the core of the Internet experience. The balancing act continues, but in my estimation, there have been enough successes, and failures in this time period to have an outline of what will work and what will not work.

Knowing your strengths and weaknesses is evidence of maturity. In 2019, we have a much more realistic conception of the strengths and weaknesses of the Internet. Internet Maturity is also evident in how people more frequently use it to facilitate activities in person.

People now use the Internet to facilitate activities in person far more than the first phases of the Internet 1995-2015. People continue to use social media to blast out one-directional rants, pictures, videos, and memes to the world, many of which the world would rather not see. But people are also using social media to communicate through voice, video, and text with timing and a depth of emotion enhancing both in-person and Internet interactions.

Internet maturity does imply some degree of stability in the use and functionality of technology. It also assumes widespread knowledge of using the tools and a degree of trust, which may not last, in letting the Internet be more fully integrated into every facet of our lives. The Internet is more often the means of arriving at the destination, not the destination itself, as it was in the '90s.

As I have asserted many times in this book, the Internet is increasingly intuitive and natural for people born each year after the early '90s. Each year, the values, culture, and effects of Internet information saturation are more deeply enmeshed in our collective mindset. In the early years, there was a lengthy period to adapt to the Internet, and the consequent social and mental isolation was harsh at times. The isolation, awkwardness, and randomness of the Internet common in many interactions between 1995–2015 (roughly) have diminished, albeit gradually.

What Does Google Say About That?

It is Google that most often prioritizes information and influences the relevance it has for us, individually and societally. People born after the early '90s generally grew up knowing the Internet as being fun, functional, and a defining part of the future. And when they entered High School, Google was in wide use, overtaking books and libraries as primary sources. Anyone in college after about 2005, likely consulted Google much more frequently than a library.

To find an answer, people Google, check Wikipedia, or in the past 10 years, crowdsourcing on social networking sites like Facebook and LinkedIn or other online fora has become more useful. People have been generally so amazed at the reality of fast, and reliable, information that only in recent years have people asking more questions about the negatives.

Easily attained information can easily trick your brain into thinking knowledge is easily attained. Just finding a fact can make people feel they deserve all the respect as someone who did the hard work of thinking, studying, researching, missing, failing, and then finally succeeding in pinning down the correct information or insight. Acquiring information doesn't include the patience and discernment to appropriately use it.[100]

Due to fewer people online in the late '80s through the late '90s, it was harder then than it is today to find their group of people on the Internet. It could work great, and give you a distinct advantage since few people had access. But for many people there first few times online felt like entering a vast unpredictable wasteland. The content was often not vetted or organized. During this time, most people found the Internet to be slow and unreliable.

Between 1995 through 2015 society was experiencing growing pains of the changing digital landscape. Time was necessary for technology to improve but what is often overlooked is how people needed time to adjust socially.

People born in the early '90s have a full life span of memories that involved the Internet in some way. The lines distinguishing friends they met in real life and those from the Internet are less concrete than older generations. My younger siblings and younger friends are far more comfortable with who they meet online than those just a few years older. This digital dividing line has created deep distinctions in

---

[100] I do not want to imply that truth and information can only be encountered in a hard way. This is more of a warning to avoid succumbing to the arrogance of thinking just because you know something doesn't ensure you understand it well enough to know what to do with it. Easily findable facts have had this effect on generations growing up with the Internet.

how each generation socializes. This is why it represents the most significant intergenerational differences in lifestyle and opinions since WW II.

For many born in the '70s and before, they never became immersed in the culture of the Internet at a young enough age to have it affect them like those born in the '80s or the '90s. It was not a part of their social experience in High School and they could put it off. For those of us born in the '80s, we had no choice, we were educationally, socially, culturally, and professionally compelled to use, understand, and be well versed on the Internet.

Many in older generations would dismiss the early Internet with comments like "it's not for me, I'm from a different generation" and if you were old enough you could basically get away with that. I have seen many older academics get away with mostly using the Internet for email, and an occasional search, meanwhile younger staff had to become better versed and immersed in all forms of internet communication and social networking.

Those born in the '80s grew up seeing the Internet developing into its relatively mature phase today. We watched the Internet come of age as our minds and bodies were simultaneously going through a similar process. We are an "In-Between" generation because we could never fully settle on pre-Internet or post-Internet culture and mentality.

In the more mature Internet phase, people view the Internet as a constant. It facilitates and enhances social interactions, both with friends that you also interact with in real life, and many others that know, primarily, through a screen. While I do believe the Internet experience will never quite match the reality we experience in real-life, perhaps one day the connection between our Internet life and real-life will one day be near seamless.

CHAPTER THIRTEEN

OTHER WAYS THE INTERNET CHANGED US

Meeting, Flirting, Dating, Marrying

In 2006 my roommate Zach and I discussed how online dating was becoming quite normal. In the '90s and early '00s there was a persistent stigma that people who met online to date or get married were weird or had limited social skills. By 2006 this stigma was fading fast, especially among younger people. At the time, Zach and I anticipated that within 10 years meeting someone online to date would be nearly as common and socially acceptable as people meeting through more traditional means (friends, work, etc.).

The Internet did impose social isolation because it made in-person socializing, especially for young people, less common. People crossed paths in real-life less often because they spent more time on computers and also felt less inclined to interact when they did cross paths. Real-life communication and interactions were so different and removed from online interactions at that time. This made it harder to meet people to form relationships and also disrupted existing relationships as couples experienced less, quality, face time.

New rules of dating were needed for this new reality. After some period of awkwardness, people adapted socially to the new dating rules. It took some years, but once people in large numbers began to adapt to the Internet dating reality, dating improved immensely.

Of course, as online dating became more normal there were downsides.

In 2011 I read an article online summarizing the state of online dating. The author saw that a surfeit of dating options and ease of access to meeting people online had reached a point that was making some people pickier, resulting in committed relationships becoming less appealing. The author opined that for men and women the highest priority in selecting a dating partner online was someone who would most generously give affection with the least expectation for that affection to be reciprocated.

In other words, what many were aiming for was a low-risk high-reward relationship situation. People were becoming far more risk-averse and avoided vulnerability, making real affection or true intimacy more out of reach. In these scenarios, it did feel at times like you could, in theory, date any person you wanted unless, of course, you actually liked them. Really liking someone would imply you expected commitment and reciprocation from the other person. Feeling commitment and reciprocation would, of course, involve feeling vulnerable and people were very very averse to making themselves vulnerable or showing they cared.

Being ghosted (not getting any response) became much more frequent after 2008. It coincided with a rise in mobile phones and people receiving messages on different devices at all hours of the day, and not remembering which medium to respond with. Sometimes people didn't even mean to ghost someone, just with so much activity on one device and limited time to strain the eyeballs and focus on one thing made it hard to come up with clever responses. Many potential dating relationships tapered off after a missed text or phone call. Many people, more often men than women, were left in the dark, wondering why they got ghosted, explaining the situation to friends, but nobody ever knew.

Over time the solution to the social isolation imposed by early Internet usage was in getting more people online and improving those interactions. As more people used the Internet and Internet dating apps, the quality of the apps improved and the interactions improved. Stigma would persist but just as more people use a product it becomes normal, so it was with dating websites and apps.

We Got Bigger, Exercise and Body Image

Growing up in the '80s and '90s, most comments regarding body size focused on how much taller and stronger people were today compared with previous generations and medieval times, due to improved nutrition. By the late '90s, the commentary shifted as Americans came to be recognized for, and unconcerned with, their bloated bodies while visiting prominent tourist sites in countries around the world. Increased economic prominence enabling world leisure travel also made it easier to grow in body size.

Since 1975,[101] the global obesity rate has nearly tripled, with nearly 2 billion overweight or obese worldwide. 1975 is significant because it is one of the last years before computers or the Internet had any significant impact on our body sizes. Since the mid-'90s, when Internet use started to become normal, obesity rates have continued to climb throughout the world.

Roughly correlating with the rise in the use of computers and the Internet, commentary shifted from how much healthier people were compared with previous generations to how relatively out of shape we were becoming. As Internet culture stretched across the world most, but not all, countries followed a similar pattern of expanding body sizes.

Contrary to what it was like in the '80s or '90s, oversized bodies are far from being a US phenomenon. By 2013,[102] Mexico had surpassed the US as the world's most obese country. By 2015, the US had long since lost its position as the world's most obese country, falling to 12th place. The sedentary lifestyle accompanying the Internet is likely the biggest single factor in increasing rates of obesity.

---

[101] Obesity rates have become a significant public health issue for many countries:
https://www.who.int/news-room/fact-sheets/detail/obesity-and-overweight
https://www.ncbi.nlm.nih.gov/pmc/articles/PMC4216968/
https://www.nytimes.com/interactive/2017/09/16/health/brazil-obesity-nestle.html
https://www.telegraph.co.uk/news/health/news/3342882/Japanese-get-a-taste-for
-Western-food-and-fall-victim-to-obesity-and-early-death.html
[102] https://www.actigraphcorp.com/news-article/mexico-surpasses-u-s-as-worlds-fattest
-nation/

Living through this period of increased Internet usage, you could see and feel the difference in your body. The Internet made it so you really noticed the difference of not getting enough exercise, and it really required that you make a conscious effort to get in shape. There began to be a real distinction between those who took health and exercise seriously and those who were not able or didn't want to.

To add to all this, self-consciousness amplified with the use of social media projecting the image of the ideal face and body at the very same time that Internet use was increasing obesity. Everyone constantly had images in front of them comparing themselves to everyone else in every aspect whether it was fair or not.

Internet use and an accompanying sedentary lifestyle was likely the largest single contributor to obesity in this time period. But it wasn't the only factor and it is difficult to parse out the exact drivers in rising obesity. The '80s, '90s, '00s, and '10s were loaded with TV viewing, video game use, more sedentary forms of employment, and much of this change was attributable to the Internet.

The major benefit of our current environment, that's often overlooked, is that the Internet provides easy access to health information incomparable with any previous time period. Although Doctors and nutritionists may never admit this, the abundance of health information available today can allow many people to take better care of themselves, in most situations, better than trained professionals could just ten or twenty years ago. Furthermore, there have been some notable Internet entrepreneurs, like Michael Dell, who turned into health advocates drawing attention to more healthy living.

The Internet is now a key source for improving education in dietary habits, exercise, and other healthy lifestyle options. But this information still must be handled with discernment, judgment, and a strong understanding of basic health principles, Understanding Internet sales and marketing techniques is useful to ascertain whether someone is genuinely trying to inform or just sell some new trend diet. Consequently, I do not anticipate the demand or need for trained health professionals to diminish anytime soon.

Managing Your Personal Brand

In 2007, I came across a YouTube channel episode hosted by Zadi Diaz explaining that people comparing themselves to models in magazines was unrealistic due to digital enhancements modifying every photograph.[103] Since 2007, digital enhancement has become the norm. Digital photo retouching has become a growing freelance business.

Constantly being compared to others for how we look, what we represent, and generally being judged on social media or dating apps by a single photo or phrase we say have all contributed to making us more conscious of our online image. To combat some of the pains from being judged we avail ourselves to an array of apps and app features to improve our image.

Beginning in late 2012, I noticed people began to specify #nofilter to indicate the realness and natural beauty of photos. Authenticity was beginning to be viewed as a way to make up for perceived shortcomings. It was a reminder that people were becoming increasingly aware of how everything on the Internet was looking more altered, unnatural, and fake.

A Chinese company named Meitu is one of the largest tech companies in the world, and it has various beauty enhancement apps. In mid-2019, Meitu apps had been downloaded on over a billion devices.[104]

Looking back, altering or enhancing your appearance has always been a key appeal of the Internet. Many chat rooms and websites in the early years required, not your real name, but an alias or avatar. Having a personality that was different from what you lived in real life was an appealing and even exciting part of the Internet to some people.

During this period there was also a significant increase in plastic surgery in many different countries.[105] Filters, digital photo retouching,

---

[103] The 2017 book *Fantasyland*, by Kurt Andersen, informed some of this thinking here on the globally increasing popularity of plastic surgery and other forms of altering one's appearance to fit with increasingly unreal expectations.

[104] https://en.wikipedia.org/wiki/Meitu

[105] https://globenewswire.com/news-release/2018/03/01/1402022/0/en/New-Statistics-Reveal-the-Shape-of-Plastic-Surgery.html

and increased social networking likely contributed to increasing demand for a permanently improved look. As your online identity became more seamless and synced up with who you are in real life there was a huge rise in popularity of apps to enhance your image, and some people took the need for enhancement quite seriously.

Selfies and Instagram

While visiting Venice in 2017, I decided to step away from some of the huge crowds down a secluded alleyway into a semi-secluded dock area along one of the many scenic canals. As I walked up it was vacant, but within the next couple minutes, several groups of tourists entered, snapped a photo, and left. One girl who was about 25 entered with a couple friends. She immediately walked to the edge of the dock, made a pose by spreading her arms out and then, speaking to her friends, loudly demanded: "make sure you get the best Instagram photo of your whole life!" They snapped several photos, examined them, and about 30 seconds later disappeared down the alleyway and into the crowds.

Between 2011–2018, at least 259 deaths were directly attributed to taking a selfie, according to one study.[106] As selfies became more popular, you could notice a change as people cared less about experiencing the place and more about the response to the social media response. Usually, people just copied what they saw someone else do in an Instagram selfie. It has likely diminished our awareness and ability to perceive our surroundings.

With Instagram everyone became an amateur photographer imitating professional photographers. Instagram made exceptional use of filters to accentuate moods or feelings for every photo, whether real or feigned. Since social media companies often succeed inasmuch as they drive emotions the photo filters driving emotions are essential to its success.

Instagram also seemed to always push the most captivating and emotionally manipulative photos (awe, jealousy, vanity, lust) to the top.

---

[106] The mean age was 22.94 years old, 72.5% males and 27.5% female. *Journal of Family Medicine and Primary Care*, Jul-Aug 2018. https://www.ncbi.nlm.nih.gov/pmc/articles/PMC6131996/

As Instagram became saturated with seemingly amazing photos promoting ideal, even if not real, lifestyles people flocked to the same to copy, mimic, emulate those ideals lifestyles. Instagram was wisely purchased by Facebook early on, as it was replacing Facebook as the new cool social networking platform that people trusted and felt comfortable interacting not just with your friends but with strangers as well. Instagram has remained the friendliest social media platform. The core struggle of Instagram is between authenticity and clicks. Photos are often near-identical, following the same trends and patterns because familiarity often drives more traffic than authenticity. The same target moods and inspirational quotes were reused over and over. After 2018, Instagram began to feel quite repetitive, like you were seeing the same photo a hundred times over, just with a different person or slightly different caption. In time, just a small share of photos had any unique meaning because most were just replicating a thought, feeling, or spiritual symbolism you had seen in hundreds of photos.

Meeting People Changed

Meeting spontaneously through chance encounters has certainly declined since the Internet. For example, I don't hear of people just bumping into someone on the street and then chatting for an hour or people becoming friends with someone while waiting for a bus or outside a concert venue. But I do hear stories of people becoming friends after renting out an Airbnb room in their house.

Chance encounters like bumping into people on the street or getting a date after meeting in the checkout line have declined. But meeting people through a variety of online channels has gone way up. Many friendships formed through a first contact online are the result of people purposefully trying to meet someone, but not always. Social networking has been a big facilitator. I remember back in 2011 being a meeting and discussing people for potential positions. Someone said, "you know, just looking at someone's Facebook page is usually more helpful to find out who they are than talking with them."

Social networking is very useful to get a sense of people. The downside is that in assuming that everything is locatable online, people have also declined in the ability to find out information directly from the person and distinguish nuance and specifics from vague generalities.

Traveling international, I have seen many instances where people assume they know everything about someone based solely on the country of origin. The ease of knowledge available online has perhaps tricked many of us into assuming we know more than we do. We have become accustomed to finding everything online and doing little deep thinking.

Learning

We may be just beginning to grasp the full potential of online learning. Till now, it has been mostly used as a supplement to formal education. In the early years, it was frustrating how slowly the Internet was effective used to educate. At the University level, professors and administrators gave some resistance to the Internet.

Part of this may have been that some older professors and administrators were, due to the generational gap, far less comfortable than their students at using the Internet. But another part seemed to be the worry by professors and university administrators that the Internet could disrupt their whole business model.

Between 2000–2006, I remember reading in so many college textbooks that would explain some theory or research and then conclude, "However, this [insert topic] is changing due to the Internet, and only in the upcoming years will the outcomes of these changes be determined."

The textbook authors were effectively kicking the can 5–10 years down the road rather than offering any real guidance on how to deal with education in the post-Internet world. This is true to form, the academy is rarely the most cutting edge, particularly when it comes to technology. The academic establishment prefers consensus opinions to non-vetted ideas, and finds comfort in abstraction rather than run the risk of being proven wrong. Not surprisingly, when it came to the Internet many universities fell behind the curve.

What was clear to those in university in the early '00s is that you would need to learn to adapt to this new Internet structured world and this information would be found largely outside of University textbooks and courses. On University campuses between the late '90s through the mid-'00s you always heard people say, "The internet will change that" as a catchall term for not having a real answer.

In the past few years, I have spoken with a lot of people who learn a great deal online. Many of the ideas in this book have been informed and supported by online information. Beginning around 2014, I heard countless, non-tech, people praise how some YouTube video saved them hours fixing a previously time-consuming problem on their car or finally understanding why World War I happened. In many countries around the world, informal online education, through many sites, is a wellspring of information where access to good educational materials is limited, non-existent, or cost-prohibitive.

I have spoken to International students at Universities who said, "Wikipedia is better at explaining these topics in class than the professor." The growing potential for Internet learning is still enormous and it appears we are on the cusp of massive growth in online education.

VHS Tapes, DVDs, Blue Ray

A girl I met while traveling in Portugal told me a story about VHS tapes from when she was 15. She said that she repeatedly watched a scene from the film *Assassins* on a VHS cassette. She shared how she really liked the scene where Antonio Banderas emerges from a house looking really cool. She rewound the VHS tape so many times to re-watch that one scene that she broke the VHS tape.

One reason nobody misses VHS tapes is the physical limitations on those VHS tapes such as breaking when rewinding, or how hard it was to rewind or fast-forward the VHS. I can't remember the last time I used a VHS tape. I almost never see VHS tape collections in people's homes. In the early '00s, these were replaced by DVD's, since DVD's were far more convenient and higher quality.

But once streaming came along and then high-speed broadband Internet allowed for near equal viewing quality people made the switchover relatively easy.

By around 2010 you could stream most movies, TV shows, and music online. Since there was no physical purchase of the entertainment content, there was a feeling that it was all easily replaceable. People began to have less attachment to the specific movie or TV show and the values it expressed and became more concerned with the entertainment value it provided and the feelings it generated.

In the '90s people could quote music and movies all the time. But by the late '00s people quoted less and remembered less because if they needed to, they could just look up a song or movie clip online. The ease of access to any content at any time reduced our need to remember or become attached.

New Ways to Organize

In late 2012, I moved to Washington DC and when I arrived I used Meetup.com to find stuff to do. Meetup.com worked like an online billboard where people could post events. The events could be a networking event, a language group, a volleyball match, etc. I found several meetup groups for Ultimate Frisbee.

Meetup had been popular since around 2005 but by 2013 it seemed to be losing ground in popularity. One reason was that the meetup updates were sent only to your email only and at a time when people were getting overloaded with emails making Meetup seem like spam. People in the group made updates sporadically and most people in the group felt out of the loop.

By 2014, several people, who were in their mid-30s, that had been sending the updates through Meetup handed it off to a guy who was about 25. Immediately he switched from Meetup to Facebook to send out ultimate Frisbee game status updates. People could check the updates easily and regularly since they were often checking Facebook anyway.

Soon after, game sizes doubled and then tripled, and the quality of play and skill also improved. The frequency of fights and arguments on the field went down too. The pool of people on the Facebook group soon surpassed 500. New Ultimate Frisbee players began showing up at games saying they found the group by just searching on Facebook for Frisbee groups in DC.

This example illustrates the more efficient ways of communicating through social networking tools as well as the generational divide with new technology. For organizing events in real-time, the social media updates were far superior to blasting out emails because as many people could follow the updates as wanted to follow. No surprise social media was instrumental in protests and other mass organized demonstrations and events all over the world.

Seeking Real Emotions in Real Life
Living more and more inside screens has distanced the emotional experience from real-life. Anyone who lived through this can probably think of many instances where the life they lived and experienced is not what was represented online. Sometimes the Internet was a conduit into the real-life we thought we should be living because that appeared better than the reality we lived.

Many videos on social media that went viral after 2015 were promoted with a tagline similar to: "Bradley Cooper, gets emotional talking about his life growing up" or "Jennifer Lawrence cries when asked about the personal toll of her latest movie role" or "Dave Grohl finally opens up about … " It was like media was just reacting to reactions and this was all they needed to promote something and attract people's attention.

For many people, viewing people's reactions online was a substitution for diminishing frequency or intensity of emotional experiences in their own life. Watching videos, or seeing GIFs of reactions online through a screen at least drove some emotional feeling. Displaying emotions was a good way to get clicks since it was usually the quickest and most convincing method to convey a truth or promote some story or myth.

Ironically, the more that people had access to everyone all the time, the more people showed more need for genuine personal connection and deep emotional experiences.

Nevertheless, improvements in technology appear capable of improving the social situation. Some of the emotional distance could be attributed to social adaptation and the rugged tools we have used to connect online. As the tools improve and we become more adapted to those improvements the overall experience will improve after periods of adjustment.

CHAPTER FOURTEEN

THE FUTURE

It is often the case that our personal strengths and talents are the same that also comprise, in their extreme, our greatest personal flaws. The same can be said of the Internet. During the first wave of internet discovery (roughly 1995–2010), there was near-universal amazement and optimism in what the Internet could do. As it continued to touch more aspects of our lives the downsides become more obvious and easier to manage.

A concept articulated repeatedly in Nassim Taleb's 2012 book *Antifragile* asserts that in regards to dealing with adverse scenarios in life, preparation is far more beneficial than precisely anticipating how and when negative events will occur. In other words, both at the individual and societal level, we are better off spending more time strengthening ourselves to handle difficult scenarios than obsessively predicting what exactly will happen. In this spirit, these plausible future scenarios are shared, for preparatory purposes rather than precise prediction.

Rebalancing of Societal Politics

As stated at the outset of this book, the boomer generation has been exceptionally successful in unifying their political interests. They elected three presidents that were all born at the very beginning of the baby boom. Though it is possible that the first generation born with the Internet may garner significant political clout, it is also possible that the fracturing of interests caused by the deluge of information online creates an environment much harder to focus on common issues.

The boomers lived through an era where they were fed by big media. This helped them to adhere to mainstream cultural tastes. Perhaps, the political cohesion the boomers had will not be replicated in the near future. There are just too many preferences, choices, values, to find a common theme or topic.

In the United States, 2016, was a major election cycle where the Internet was the most mature it had ever been and it was the dominant form of conveying information. Each new medium, whether books, newspapers, radio, has, in turn, led to a better-informed populace which over time. Most assume that this pattern of better-informed and educated population will continue with the Internet. As stated throughout this book, this may be the case long-term but it may still take more time for the benefits to be realized.

For much of the '90s and '00s, it was well understood that the Internet would increase access to knowledge and make it harder for governments or corporations to control information. During this period, people could foresee that changes were coming. The excitement and exuberance of the perceived positive changes overshadowed the negative possibilities brought on by the Internet.

By the year 2000, few could have predicted how, or when, this change would have occurred. Beginning with Barack Obama in 2008, the presidential victor has been the one who communicates best online and harnesses the Internet's potential most effectively. This pattern continued in 2012, and 2016, and in many elections around the world.

How will politics change with more people who grew up with the Internet holding a political office? It is likely that many things will not change, but it will be harder to achieve and maintain consensus on any issue.

Continual Conflicts Over Data Management

The exchange we are making for using online services free of charge is that we, and the data we offer, become the product.[107] The Anthony

---

[107] I attribute this idea to Roger McNamee. He made this comment in an interview that I saw in an online video sometime between 2010–2012. I tried to find the video but was unable to locate it.

Snowden Data Breach in 2013, and numerous data breaches since have revealed gaping vulnerabilities of governments and businesses in storing personal information. This tension and struggle will continue for years. It will be fought between countries, between companies, and between individuals.

The Snowden data breach and the Cambridge Analytica[108] data breach in 2015 were watershed moments. Silicon Valley began to be viewed differently by outsiders, and for the first time began to itself differently. Many media outlets in the US and western countries began to view tech companies with increased skepticism and heightened scrutiny in their use of data and privacy.

Since 2013, most of us have received emails from companies stating how our data was compromised by a data breach. The email usually includes a template apology, followed by some vague assurance not to worry as company X is very concerned for your safety, blah, blah, blah.

It appears that the real reason that most of these hacks don't amount to much is because it is a lot easier to steal a bunch of data than to do something with much of it. Few individuals involved in a data breach are likely to be directly impacted. It is fairly easy to collect, harder to protect, but even harder to effectively use the data once stored. The thing is enormity of the data often makes it equally hard to use it for either good or bad purposes but hcks will become more targeted and sophisticated.

Countries with Best Coding Capabilities Most Likely to Succeed

The countries that have fared best economically in the Internet Era are those with competitive advantages in coding, information technology, and related disciplines. These also tend to be the countries with strong educational foundations extending back hundreds of years and invested considerably in developing technological infrastructure.

Technical advantages afforded by the collection and use of data are likely on par to become what aircraft, heavy artillery, and nuclear weapons were in the last century in terms of strategic importance.

---

[108] https://www.theguardian.com/technology/2018/jul/11/facebook-fined-for-data-breaches-in-cambridge-analytica-scandal

Growing City State Dynamics

While in Kyiv, Ukraine in 2017, I met a girl who worked for Microsoft. We spoke about the job market for people with education and skills. With a mixture of gratitude and anxiousness, she expressed how the IT sector in Ukraine was viewed as an economic saving grace. The one piece of the economy going well. It provided a decent base of good-paying jobs propping up a historically fragile economy struggling with the competitive realities of globalization. Throughout the world, there are countries, states, and cities, and people, desperate for these good IT sector jobs.

As cities in the US, and around the world, become more specific and anxious in seeking long-term economic vitality, they will likely become more deliberate, or desperate, in competing to get the right people to fill those coveted jobs. As there are expected to be fewer jobs created than in previous waves of Industrial change, which places get the jobs will often be pivotal. Cities will expand efforts in attracting people with specific skill sets and lifestyles, for both economic and political motives.

The concept of a sanctuary city has expanded significantly in the US in recent years. Not surprising, major tech hubs like San Francisco and Seattle have led the way in adamantly affirming the values they espouse by declaring who they want to make feel welcome. To a casual observer, it appears something like echoes city-states exercising greater control and autonomy. Cities are becoming more assertive in selecting which federal laws and policies they will comply with.

This may just be the latest of the greater urban-rural divide building for centuries. But increasingly there is less mutual concern and connectedness between those in metropolitan areas and everywhere else. I have heard multiple times when people declare how little they care about anything happening 25 miles outside their metropolitan area. People increasingly see little need or importance for areas not similar to or directly tied to their immediate city system.

If the social fabric continues to fray due to fewer meaningful jobs evenly distributed in many regions, cities on the losing end will be more compelled to appeal more strongly to people with the skill sets they most need. As political values have more infused themselves into the workplace and attached themselves to certain industries cities may try to attract and accommodate workers by choosing which federal laws not to uphold based on the jobs they need. Over time this will likely come from all political sides and perspectives and various shapes and sizes.

Lower taxes, social benefits, environmental conditions, city layout, and approach to drug policies are all issues that cities have used in the past to attract people with different priorities and interests. Many billionaires disproportionately live in places like San Francisco and New York, the very cities with the highest tax rates.[109] As conditions change, some cities with few billionaires and high net-worth individuals may try to become a safe-haven for billionaires by better catering to their needs as they may become targets of scorn. Other cities will likely pursue very obvious campaigns and tactics to attract people in the IT sector, or people that they feel would best complement their style, culture, and economy.

Politicizing Tech Companies

Technological innovation is a big part of what advances a society. There is a real risk of overly politicizing the creative process in technology. As tech companies have become more profitable, larger, and more entrenched in society they are susceptible to broader societal political influence.

This approach runs counter to the problem-solving attitude and think-outside-the-box mindset that was a necessary ingredient to the Internet Revolution. Many of the people in Silicon Valley that brought about the major successes seemed to have had persistence in their pursuit of truth or finding a better way. Many of these people were those that were shunned or ignored by mainstream society until they achieved large salaries and stock options.

---

[109] Enrico Moretti's 2012 book, *The New Geography of Jobs*, has excellent graphs, maps, and data explaining why jobs are located where they are and where job growth will occur.

Soren Kierkegaard stated:

"Truth always rests with the minority, and the minority is
always stronger than the majority, because the minority
is generally formed by those who really have an opinion,
while the strength of a majority is illusory, formed by the
gangs who have no opinion—and who, therefore, in the
next instant (when it is evident that the minority is the
stronger) assume its opinion ... while truth again reverts to
a new minority."[110]

Startup workers, innovative engineers, and other creative personalities are often the personalities trying to apply truth to fix a
problem that most in society either cannot see or cannot solve. Inject-
ing politics into the process of research, discovery, and new thinking
almost always stifles the best ideas. It can also repel the happy few
individuals looking for deeper truths and bigger solutions that tran-
scend petty politics, which would be a significant loss.

Tech companies are not set up to be political entities. Generally,
the further they stay away from politics the better. Societies are
immensely complex, with so many facets of industry, cultural myths,
behavioral customs, social habits, educational roots, and legal codes
that all somehow blend together. Tech companies, by virtue of creating successful products are currently generating the most new wealth
in society, do not necessarily have the foundation or moral authority
to suggest they are best equipped to fix or manage the complexity of
societies' concerns.

They are free to dabble, try, and contribute what they can, but
should not be given excessively preferential treatment by virtue of
accomplishments in unaffiliated domains. Leaders, or workers, in an
industry with rapidly increasing societal influence, such as the tech
sphere, should exercise extreme caution in assuming success in one

---

[110]This quote is from *The Diary of Soren Kierkegaard*, published by Citadel in 1960.

area guarantees success in unrelated and sensitive areas of society. Thus, politicizing tech companies should be avoided.

Real World Merging with Internet World

As stated at the outset of this book, the first step in technological change is creating the tools. The second step, which is absolutely essential, is for society to collectively learn how to use and adapt to the consequences of tools. This second step ultimately determines how fun, exciting, societally enriching, and socially rewarding the new tech reality will be for each generation. We ultimately decide what this will look like, not the technology.

The Internet World is merging more closely with the Real World. Our identity, behavior, and habits are likely to more closely mirror who we are in both worlds. As we improve our ability to convey and receive human expressions through the Internet, in consequence the reality experienced by each generation will be altered to create a new version of real-life.

'90s Music, Values, Internet, and Technology

"Goodnight to the Rock 'n' Roll era
Cause they don't need you anymore"[III]
— Stephen Malkmus, from indie rock band Pavement

The 90s is remembered for its music. Since I often meet people around the world interested in the music from this period I have included this "bonus" section. Additionally, because modern music and the Internet appealed to young people, the Internet had an early and acute impact on the creation, production, and distribution of music. Arguably, the Internet affected the music world more quickly and thoroughly than any entertainment industry.

INTERNET KILLED THE RADIO STAR

Radio was vital to youth culture in the '80s and early '90s. Music and ideas spread through radio and powerfully influenced culture and what was cool. The teenage years are very important as it is often in this period when our minds are most open to new music which in turn shapes our personality for a long time. Radio played a critical role in this process.

Actor Michael Fassbender, who was a teenager in the early '90s, shared this about the important role music played in cultivating your personal identity:

[III] Lyrics to song, "Fillmore Jive" on the album, *Crooked Rain, Crooked Rain*, released in February 1994.

166

"Nowadays, people just listen to everything, it's great, but
back when I was at school, high school, you were a goth or
you were into grunge or you were into punk or you were
into metal and that kind of defined your style in what you
wore and the groups you hung out with"[112]

In Seattle in the '90s, there were several rock stations, 107.7FM
The End (Alternative Rock), 99.9KISW (Classic and Heavy Rock), 90.3
KEXP (College radio, Indie, and Experimental Rock). There was a popular R&B station called 93.3 (The KUBE) and Top 40 station, 106.1 (KISS).
The University of Washington and a few colleges and high schools
in the area had small radio stations run by students at their schools.
These smaller stations had very few listeners. Fewer listeners usually
implied greater freedom to play newer, less commercial, and edgier
music. There were a few stations that played oldies which included
music from iconic groups that retained their coolness for decades (The
Doors, Led Zepellin, The Beatles, and The Rolling Stones.)

By the late 90s, Disc Jockey's (DJs) were fading fast in their relevancy. For decades DJs guided what music was cool. Work that was traditionally done by DJs, like song selection, was becoming automated.
DJs no longer had as much control and were not the connoisseurs of
music they had been for previous generations.

Some DJs around this time did try to stay connected to their audiences, even personally answering phone call requests to the station. I
called in several times to 107.7 The End in Seattle, the biggest alternative station in Seattle. I requested songs from the top DJs and they usually played it within a couple of hours.

In the spring of 1997, Dave Grohl, from the band the Foo Fighters,
was visiting the station of 107.7 The End to promote their new album
The Color and the Shape.

---

[112] Michael Fassbender, quoted by metalinjection.com Sep 10, 2014. http://metalinjection
.net/metal-in-the-mainstream/actor-michael-fassbender-aka-magneto-is-a-metalhead

Grohl and his band were on-air with DJ Marco Collins trying to figure out where people could find a rare b-side song called "How I Miss You" that was released a couple of years prior. Grohl wasn't exactly sure which released single the song was on. I knew the answer so I called into the station about 10 times and got the busy signal every time.

I was shocked when eventually one of the calls I made went through and I heard a voice answer and say, "Hold, please." On live radio I nervously explained, "Hi, guys, the song 'How I Miss You' is actually on the 'Big Me' Single" without hesitation Dave Grohl responded "Oh, it is the 'Big Me' single? Cool, thanks for letting us know" After a few more words I was off. Grohl was a busy guy, recording albums and touring, and he probably didn't keep track of all songs B-Side releases.

I was just 15, so it felt pretty cool to be talking to one of the coolest bands of that time. Radio stations still felt personal and connected to their home cities.

Up until the mid-'90s most cities had local radio stations that were still independent or in other words not controlled by a centralized national corporation. Most of the DJs and staff at radio stations in the '90s had worked at college radio stations in the '80s, a period in which avante garde and independent (indie) music was cool and anything popular or commercialized was not.

The homegrown music scenes in cities like Minneapolis, Boston, Cleveland, Seattle were very local. Economics was a factor, you could live cheap in those cites in the '80s and early '90s. Chris Cornell, from Soundgarden, said in a podcast interview[113] that in the early '80s he held many low skill jobs like "cleaning and gutting fish and waiting tables" that paid the bills and also allowed him the mental freedom to work on songs in his head. Living downtown was far less expensive than the highly gentrified cities loaded with new real estate developments today.

The bands that played in the late '80s, and would later define much of the alternative rock scene of the '90s, performed a balancing act. Band members of Pearl Jam, Nirvana, Smashing Pumpkins, and

---

[113] Marc Maron WTF podcast interview with Chris Cornell from June 2014.

The Red Hot Chilli Peppers were famous for making public statements vilifying "sellout" bands or those whose objective in music was simply becoming rich and famous. Nevertheless, all the big bands played the game of success with lucrative recording contracts, MTV, extensive radio play, and publicity.

It was uncomfortable to watch '90s rock stars like Eddie Vedder (Pearl Jam), John Frusciante (RHCP), and Kurt Cobain (Nirvana) lash out at journalists about big crowds and not liking the public spotlight. Much of their persona and values came from '80s punk rock ethos, which was better suited to smaller, more personalized, music communities.

The pejorative term "sellout" was so common throughout interviews with musicians of the time. Bands would attack other bands for getting famous, usually out of jealousy. If you read interviews with bands in the early to mid-'90s you could tell there was a shift in mindset. Most of the artists were adapting to leaving their smaller and more artistic communities for bigger audiences, which meant creating new relationships and ending others.

It was a totally different mindset from the rock music era of the '80s when hair metal bands (Poison, Whitesnake, Bon Jovi) sought to strongly convey an appearance of success. Many '90s bands actively sought to avoid any appearance of success. Ambivalence to fame or attention was, in the '90s, a way of displaying your success.

But due to human nature, as some bands became successful and others didn't, jealousies flared. Bands were always attacking other bands. It was a competition of being cool, holding the public's attention and having the leverage to do what you wanted creatively.

But there was a change happening. The wave of wealth and changing social behaviors brought on by the Internet beginning in the mid-90s began to manifest. By the late '90s, the economy and attitudes changed drastically. The pejorative term "sellout" mostly vanished, and there was no shame in overtly seeking success.

By the '00s, creative value and integrity were valued less than strict success based on numbers. The wisdom of crowds, going viral, receiving the most clicks and "likes" was how people defined value and relevance in the Internet world. Artistic creativity as being valuable in and

of itself was an afterthought or ignored completely. People often more
callously used these measures to define the value of people.

There was a noticeable effect on music. By the late '90s, people
were far less interested in listening to music about pain, loneliness, or
hopelessness. Also, due to the changes brought about by the economy
and the Internet, there were not as many people that could authenti-
cally sing, write, or perform music that expressed those feelings. The
economy had improved, and many would-be musicians, they found
stable jobs instead of writing songs.

In this time the new creative energies began shifting towards
digital platforms. Many of the creative types moved into more lucrative and increasingly tech-heavy careers in web design or User Experience design. To be creative you were required to learn to be creative
on a digital, more Internet-friendly, platform. Many people in the
in-between generation did not make this transition well. They either
had started to develop their skills on platforms that were quickly
becoming obsolete, or they had not enough time early in their career
to develop their skills on the new digital platforms.

One example that illustrates this change from manual to digital
is the inspiration for the cover of this book. The guitar was for decades
a powerful medium for creative expression. Guitar music remained
dominant from the '60s and on through the '90s. But beginning in the
late '90s guitar began to be supplanted by digital instrumentation to
create music.

Guitar music has since moved further away from being central to
most modern music. The cover of this book shows a guitar shattering
into pieces that are portrayed as laptops and smartphones. This represents the creative process moving away from manual instruments
into electronic and other digital instruments.

In 1996, 107.7 The End, the Seattle alternative radio station, was
purchased by Entercom, the second-largest radio conglomerate in the
United States. This was part of the consolidation of radio stations
occurring throughout the country, and world, at the time. "The End"
was a cutting edge station that took risks playing the newest and coolest music in the alternative rock realm. It was infamous for getting in

trouble with record labels for playing music releases from Pearl Jam and Nirvana early, infuriating music industry marketers.

Though not obvious to most listeners at the time, a key person behind the station's cutting edge approach was DJ Marco Collins. Following the merger in 1998, Collins left the station. In a 2015 documentary, Collins relates that he clashed with the new management while arguing over the artistic qualities of "Bjork." leaving shortly after.[114,115]

After Collins left 107.7 The End, the music played by the station became more bland and predictable. You would hear some staple songs from post-1991[116] bands, like Alice in Chains, Live, and Offspring throughout the day. And you would also hear the latest popular hit single of the moment. The station began to sound more and more like other stations.

This radio consolidation coincided with people listening less to music on the radio and listening to more music online. Napster got big quick, along with other online music platforms. The sound quality was not great, but it was free and didn't require going to a store and spending $15 for a CD from some unproven artist.

Whether it was legal or not didn't stop most people from downloading music. People would sometimes feel a little guilty. The phrase you heard most often was "well, I got it off the Internet, I think it's legal, but I don't really know."

---

[114]As told by Marco Collins in the 2015 Amazon Prime documentary *The Glamour & the Squalor.*

[115]Interesting side note, about a year after Collins left 107.7 The End, I wandered backstage after a Modest Mouse show at the Seattle Bumbershoot festival and began talking with people. It was at the time that the Seattle band, Sunny Day Real Estate, which had a small but dedicated following, was getting back together. I made some comments about Sunny Day Real Estate visiting 107.7 The End to perform when Collins, who up until that point I just thought was some guy hanging out after the show, said: "Well, what do you think would be a cool way for them to perform a live show?" After a few minutes, I realized I was actually talking to DJ Marco Collins. I offered a few ideas off the top of my and the whole exchange was very relaxed.

[116]1991 was a big deal in the rock music world. This was the year Nirvana's album "Nevermind" was released, changing the sound of rock music. 1991 is also the year of the last Guns N' Roses studio album for years, effectively ending the big rock, hair-metal era. There was fairly strong delineation in many radio stations, the ones that mostly played post-91' music and those that played pre-'91 music.

Many felt that maybe they should be paying something for music online, but they definitely didn't want to go back to the risk of paying $15 for a CD of songs when you could just get the one or two songs you actually wanted off the Internet. Furthermore, when people enjoy a song they usually want to share it with their friends. That's what people do when they like something; they share it because it makes the whole experience more fun. And the Internet made it easier to share.

Buying Music

A young person listening to music from the '90s today may find the experience bizarre without the proper threads of music history to string together the narrative and context of the 30–40 years of musical lead up to the '90s. Previous genres of music including Blues, Jazz, Motown, Rock 'n' roll, Disco, Metal each grew out of technological advancements. The reduced cost of new technology, like electric guitars, effects pedals, synthesizers, mixing devices all triggered a change in musical style. Similarly, transistor radios, record players, cassettes and CDs all changed how and where people experienced music.

By the late '60s and early '70s, the combination of mass production, mass marketing, and greater disposable income for young people made producing and marketing music extremely profitable. At its peak, rock affiliated music generated billions of dollars of revenue in the early 1970s.

During the pre-Internet era, the music industry was largely focused on people buying a physical copy of the music, whether a record, cassette, or CD, or some other physical product related to the artist (t-shirt, poster, etc.) Before the Internet, pirating music had begun to undercut some of the music business. But pirating music was a slow process.

Around 1990–91, when I was in 3rd grade, my older brother Eric and a few of his friends started copying and then selling mix cassette tapes. Rap and R&B had just begun a big wave of popularity. Kids at school would tell us the music they wanted and then after school, we would "dub" a copy of the cassette tape onto a blank tape. It was a slow process, but good money for kids in elementary school. Some of the stuff we made copies and sold were Michael Jackson, Paula Abdul, N.W.A. Boyz 2 Men, Bell Biv De Voe.

Looking back, it seems to me that a big reason why kids at school asked us to make copies of popular music, especially the rap and hip hop groups, was that it was hard to get parents to buy a lot of this music in the store. Most of these suburban kids came from families that could well afford a $9 cassette tape.

But, in the late '80s and early '90s, there was a huge public effort to warn parents of explicit lyrics in music. I remember hearing a lot about Tipper Gore, ex-wife of former V.P. Al Gore. At the time, Tipper Gore, along with other family values activists created a public awareness campaign to pressure record labels to put warnings on music with explicit lyrics.

The large black and white warning labels on cassettes and CD's that read "explicit lyrics" made kids want to have them even more! Anything that caused your parent's concern got cooler instantly. Of course, just having a warning label was not enough, the music still had to be good, or at least a good hit song.

Why Seattle Music Became Famous in the 90s

When I lived in Denver in 1994–1996, I remember a friend asking me multiple times, "why are there so many bands from Seattle?" During the mid-'90s, the "grunge" music sound, heavily associated with Seattle, and seemed to have gotten popular everywhere.

Being in elementary school and totally unconnected to any music scene it was hard to understand what was happening with music. What I recall are phrases from people who would say things like: "Seattle is the coolest place in the country for music right now" or "Seattle is making the best music." As a kid, it seemed cool having an attachment to a city becoming more famous around the world.

I remember seeing cassette tapes and CD's of Nirvana's *Nevermind*. The cover art with all the blue water and the baby with a dollar bill, it seemed so different. That album had an enormous impact on the music world at the time and still has some cultural influence. But most kids didn't pick up on this at the time, it just seemed like something cool that was happening.

I would learn later, through MTV and VH1 music documentaries, articles in Spin, Rolling Stone, and even books[117] of how significant a change Nirvana and other Seattle groups had on music at the time.

This wave of Seattle music preceded the Internet by just a few years. It, along with gangster rap, was among the last waves of big change music that happened using the CD medium. The influence of that wave of Seattle music diminished as the Internet era took hold. Though reverberations can still be seen and heard on the Internet.

It may seem coincidental that Seattle, a mid-sized city located far from other major cities in the northwest corner of the United States, played such a pivotal role in both the technology and music of the '90s.

Was this all by chance?

The enormous flow of money Microsoft brought into the Seattle economy in the mid-'80s and early '90s played a big role. The Microsoft IPO occurred in 1986, and this created around 10,000 millionaires, including many in the Seattle area.[118] Sub Pop records, which defined the Seattle sound and released music from Soundgarden, Nirvana, and many other Seattle bands was also founded in 1988.[119]

By 1988, the Seattle music scene that became famous gathered serious momentum when the band Mudhoney released the single, "Touch Me I'm Sick", and the owners of Sup Pop records, like many tech startup workers would do in the '90s, quit their jobs to focus full time on music.[120]

---

[117] *Scar Tissue* by Anthony Kiedis brings up Nirvana throughout the book as a pivotal point in his career. *Bit of a Blur* by the bassist Alex James, brings up Nirvana several times, out of critique, and envy, but mostly highlighting how heavy an influence Nirvana was for any bands in the rock world.

[118] https://www.nytimes.com/2005/05/29/business/yourmoney/the-microsoft-millionaires -come-of-age.html

[119] https://en.wikipedia.org/wiki/Sub_Pop

[120] Ibid.

This enormous wave of tech money into the region, through Microsoft's IPO, provided capital to the region that would indirectly support the artists, musicians, and bands that a few years later would reach national and international acclaim. In some cases it was direct, Microsoft co-founder Paul Allen contributed greatly to the Seattle music scene. But often it was indirect. Most Microsoft Millionaires were not buying the music or going to the shows, but their spending did propel the economy, and they did go to restaurants where future Seattle musicians like Chris Cornell were working.

SELECTED BIBLIOGRAPHY

These books had some significant role in the thinking and ideas that went into this book. In most of these books, the authors sought in some way to understand the social, political, and cultural changes caused by technology.

1. *The World of Yesterday*, Stefan Zweig, 1941
   A memoir reflecting on the mostly overlooked interwar period leading up to World War II. Written with a heavy dose of nostalgia for what Europe was, and seemingly never could be again, it provided an excellent and authentic snapshot of what change looked and felt like before narrative historians dominate opinion.
2. *The Age of Discontinuity*, Peter Drucker, 1969
   This book has the kind of uncommon objective thinking that is needed to understand tech driven change. Drucker's assessment of change, and how humans interact remains exceptionally relevant.
3. *The Innovators Dilemma*, Clayton Christensen, 1997
   Christensen's ideas on innovation and theories greatly informed my thinking about the intersection of business, technology, and people.
4. *The Third Wave*, Alvin Toffler, 1980
   Toffler breaks down the waves of human development across the world into agricultural, industrial, and knowledge phases. Though these ideas are an oversimplification, it vastly improved my perspective on change on the global level.

5. *AntiFragile*, Nassim Taleb, 2012
   This book could well be among the most influential books of the decade. A detailed explication on becoming stronger when faced with crisis level opposition. Loaded with clever tangents and anecdotes causing me to wish I knew a lot more about everything.

6. *On War*, Carl Clausewitz, 1832
   The insights of strategy and how change occurs in this book are like nothing I've read anywhere else. There are moments of pure gold that apply to many aspects of life, not just military and politics.

7. *Ulysses*, James Joyce, 1922
   A book dealing with the big themes of cultural identity, nationalism, gender, all while living inside your own mental world is very relevant to the Internet and change happening today.

8. *Infinite Jest*, David Foster Wallace, 1996
   Loaded with information, snippets of philosophy, and tales of the highs and lows of American consumer-driven and media-saturated society. I read the book in 2015, (when the book was set to take place), and found the critiques of entertainment, addiction, advertising, achievement, and new-age psychology appropriate.

9. *The Innovators: How a Group of Inventors, Hackers, Geniuses, and Geeks Created the Digital Revolution*, Walter Isaacson, 2014
   A well-researched book on the origins of Silicon Valley companies and culture. Certainly among the best books on this topic.

10. *Fantasyland: How America Went Haywire: A 500-Year History*, Kurt Anderson, 2017
    A valuable perspective on beliefs in the United States and the changing perception of what is normal, expected, or real.

11. *Super Sad True Love Story: A Novel*, Gary Shteyngart, 2011
    Entertaining and spot on projections of the future and social dimensions of smartphone and social media use.

12. *Scar Tissue*, Anthony Keidis, 2004
    A rock star's perspective on building a worldwide fan base beyond Los Angeles confronted with changing cultural, entertainment, had a lot to say about the Internet and generational change.

ACKNOWLEDGMENTS

Special appreciation to those who were exceptionally helpful in making this book become a reality.

Will Cai, for helping form some of the core ideas from the rudimentary form to something more accurate and accessible to an audience. Doug Calhoun, for offering so many insights and perspectives to many of the stories and arguments that made into this book. Romina Staffieri, for understanding the idea, validating and supporting many of the examples from an international perspective. Ben Campbell, for excellent book recommendations and proofread help. Katarina Jambresic, for very helpful proofreading edits. My brothers Dane, Blake, and Jeff for offering opinions and examples from those a few years younger than me. Lucia Salamanca Cardona, for sharing your early chatroom life. Jeanine Rogel, for your superb teaching and offering a direct observation of kids changing in 2004–2005. Ben Brezner, for editing work and perspective on the opening chapters. Stephen Tiano, for getting the idea right away and offering professional layout expertise.

There are many, many, more people all over the world who helped in some way. It's not possible to list everyone here. But I thank and acknowledge everyone who discussed these ideas with me, contributed their opinion, offered useful criticism, and even provided their own experiences to this book.

Although I did receive help with aspects of this book, I wrote and edited most of it myself. Therefore, I accept responsibility for any errors or typos.

ABOUT THE AUTHOR

Marc grew up in Bellevue, Washington. He has lived throughout the United States (Arizona, California, Colorado, Idaho, New York, Massachusetts, and Virginia), for two years in Brazil, and traveled to over 70 countries.

In 2015, Marc began his own podcast where he interviewed a diverse array of guests, including artists, entrepreneurs, and authors. Some of the ideas about generational change and the Internet were developed through those podcast episodes.

Marc began his professional career with an internship at the United Nations and has worked in various jobs involving research and analysis at the World Bank, US Airways, and several startups.